Talking to Yourself

How Cognitive Behavior Therapy Can Change Your Life

Dr. Pamela E. Butler

iUniverse, Inc.
New York   Bloomington

Talking to Yourself
How Cognitive Behavior Therapy Can Change Your Life

The information, ideas, and suggestions in this book are not intended as a substitute for professional advice. Before following any suggestions contained in this book, you should consult your personal physician or mental health professional. Neither the author nor the publisher shall be liable or responsible for any loss or damage allegedly arising as a consequence of your use or application of any information or suggestions in this book.

iUniverse books may be ordered through booksellers or by contacting:

iUniverse
1663 Liberty Drive
Bloomington, IN 47403
www.iuniverse.com
1-800-Authors (1-800-288-4677)

Because of the dynamic nature of the Internet, any Web addresses or links contained in this book may have changed since publication and may no longer be valid. The views expressed in this work are solely those of the author and do not necessarily reflect the views of the publisher, and the publisher hereby disclaims any responsibility for them.

ISBN: 978-1-4401-1233-1 (sc)
ISBN: 978-1-4401-1234-8 (ebook)

Printed in the United States of America

iUniverse rev. date: 9/15/2009

TABLE OF CONTENTS

Acknowledgments ix

Introduction xi

1

The Judge 1

The Judgmental Structure: Drivers, Stoppers, and Confusers.
From Judge to Guide.

2

Drivers 7

Be Perfect. Hurry Up. Be Strong. Please Others. Try Hard.
Driver-Related Costs. Your Driver Profile.

3

Stoppers 19

Catastrophizing. Negative Self-Labeling. Setting Rigid
Requirements. Stopper-Related Costs. Your Stopper Profile.

4

Confusers 29

Arbitrary Negative Inferences. Positive Inferences.
Misattribution. Cognitive Deficiency. Denial.
Overgeneralization. Vague Language and Either/Or Thinking.
Magnification and Discounting. I-You Messages.

5

Changing Your Tapes. 43

The Five-Step Method. Step 1. Be Aware: "What am I telling
myself?" Step 2. Evaluate: "Is it helping?" Step 3. Identify:
"What Driver, Stopper, or Confuser is maintaining my inner
speech?"

6

The Language of Self-Support 55

Step 4. Support Yourself: "What Permission and Self
Affirmation will I give myself?" Self-Affirmation. Creating a
Buffer

7

Developing Your Guide. 69

Step 5. Develop Your Guide: "What action will I now take?"
Small Steps, Sensitivity to the Environment, Sensitivity to
Your Feelings, Sensitivity to Your Capability, Ample Reward,
Self Assertion. Summing up

8

Overcoming the Obstacles to Self-Support 85

The Second Line of Defense. Driver Interference. False
Pride.

9

Sex and Self-Talk. 91

Sex and Internal Commands. Eight Sexual Myths. Sex and
Stoppers. Sex and Self Assertion. Confronting Performance
Anxiety. Resisting Sexual Demands.

10

Talking Yourself into Anger. 105

Driver Generated Anger. Anger Generating Stoppers. The
Power of External Labels. The Effects of Internal Labels.
Letting Go. Anger Generating Confusers. A Final Word.

11

The Development of Negative Self-Talk 119

The Judge as Protector. Handing the Labels Back. Thanking
Your Judge. Discriminating Past from Present.

12

Listening to Yourself 127

Feelings, Dreams, Images, Symptoms. The Cost of Not
Listening. Taking the Leap. Accepting Others. Making the
Commitment.

Bibliography 141

ACKNOWLEDGEMENTS

This new edition of *Talking to Yourself* would not have been possible without the help and dedication of my husband, Clayton Smith. He tirelessly scanned the former edition, edited and modernized the book's language and added his own special brand of insight and clarity to the presentation. Kelly Cordellos, the wonderful personal computer whiz at Apple Computers, aided me immeasurably in creating the document that became this book. My appreciation and thanks go to Alan Salamy for the cover photograph. Ultimately, my greatest debt is to all of my clients and workshop participants over the years. Each of you taught me something about self-talk and helped me to find the keys to change it for the better.

INTRODUCTION

If you had to discover the single person in your entire life who influences you the most, who would it be? Who is the person with the greatest ability to help you or harm you? Would you choose a loving mother or father or finger an abusive and destructive parent? Would you point out a close friend or life partner or cry about the source of a broken heart?

In truth, any of these choices would be wrong. Not one comes close to the influence of the most significant being in your life, your very own self. You are your own ever-present companion. It is you who guides you. It is you who tortures you. If your inner self functions as a friend, you create an environment that helps you "trust yourself/ when all men doubt you." But if it acts as your foe, this self can push you into an abyss of despair.

This internal figure has gone by many names: superego, conscience, inner custodian, top dog, parent-part, or witch-mother. But whatever its name, you experience this inner self as a distinct person speaking to you. You engage with this person in an ever-constant dialogue, one of extreme significance. Through this internal dialogue, you make decisions and set goals for yourself, feel pleased and satisfied, or dejected and despondent. You choose to have a drink, to drive recklessly, or to tell off a friend. Or you make plans to study, to go to the gym, or to talk candidly with a loved one to clear the air. In short, you converse daily, even moment by moment, with your most valued and steadfast ally or with your most dreaded enemy.

If you have the misfortune to live with an abusive inner self, you may try to flee from this punishing, nagging companion through drugs, alcohol, promiscuity, or even through overwork. Yet, these attempts will cause more problems than they alleviate. To forego the drug or the drink or the destructive romantic encounter, you must confront the consequences of running your life according to the messages of this Imposed Self. You must face the genuine pain, sadness and rage that occur when you act against your real feelings and needs. At these moments, you will feel another self, one you have tried to subdue or even smother. This is your true authentic self and your dearest friend: the Intrinsic Self.

Listening to and honoring the Intrinsic Self is not easy. Strong rules and prohibitions get in the way. Through negative self-talk, the Imposed Self exerts itself. As one of my clients described the process: "I used to criticize myself constantly. There were no periods, semicolons, or pauses. My critic was totally pervasive. I wonder now, how did I make it through all those years?" His question is important. Many people actually perish as a result of their rigid, judgmental structures, not just through suicide, but also by the slower process of overstressing that ultimately leads to life-threatening illness.

I wrote this book to empower you to make positive changes before such catastrophes occur. Milder self-warnings can be sufficient to signal the need for change. However, if a crisis has occurred in your life to prompt you to read this book, you are in a particularly good position to alter your inner judgmental structure to make room for your true self. The Chinese character for crisis translates as either *Danger* or *Opportunity*. You can live the old adage, "More people change by feeling the heat than by seeing the light".

My goal is to help you change your self-talk, so you can enjoy an optimal level of wellbeing. I want you to have the feelings a client shared with me: "I've spent thirty-five years with a brick on my head, holding me down, and now I'm free. "

As you remove the weight of your Imposed Self and its unnecessary demands and warnings, you too will free yourself to have fun, to enjoy your life, and to connect with people who share your energy and vitality. This book seeks to connect you to your Intrinsic Self and help you to release it from it shackles.

Your exploration will go beyond that of a causal and indifferent tourist. On your journey, you will map out your relationship with your inner self. You will learn how to change your deepest psychological habits. In doing so, you will improve your life in a real and meaningful way.

CHAPTER 1

The Judge

- Do you frequently hold yourself back because you fear intruding upon other people?
- Do you believe that what you do is never enough?
- Do you need a drink or a tranquilizer in order to relax?
- Are you more forgiving of other people than you are of yourself?
- Do other people frequently disappoint you?
- Are you unable to do "nothing" and feel okay about it?
- Do you agree with the adage, "If you can't do something right, don't do anything at all?"
- Do you generally lack confidence in yourself?
- Are you often anxious, depressed, or angry?

If you answered, "yes" to these questions, you have incorporated an Imposed Self who is critical, faultfinding, and blaming. You are currently burdened by a self-monitor that sets exceedingly harsh standards and metes out equally severe penalties. Introduce yourself to your Judge.

How this Judge develops is not a mysterious process. We all begin talk to ourselves at an early age. This self-talk is based on interacting with the significant adults in our environment. Your parents' and teachers' communication with you as a child is a prototype for your later communication with yourself. If these influential people are harsh, critical, or judgmental, then your own Imposed Self will be the same. If your early mentors have realistic requirements, you learn to set achievable standards for yourself.

Based on the messages that you receive from other people, you form a self-definition, a set of controlling boundaries that determine, in large measure, your life course. You learn to see yourself as athletic or clumsy, intelligent or stupid, lovable or unlovable, okay or not okay.

Once your self-definition is formed, you will behave in a way that "proves" it true. For example, if you view yourself as a lousy athlete, you will shy away from any athletic activity. The opportunity to develop physical skills will be lost. Currently, I am working with a little boy, who has such a self-definition. He may actually be gifted physically, but he is so afraid of making mistakes that until recently, he was unwilling to toss a ball back and forth. His Judge blocked his natural ability.

Along similar lines, if you have the self-definition "I'm stupid," you will not be assertive in intellectual discussions. You will fear asking questions and therefore deprive yourself of the answers you need. I remember once visiting a chemistry professor in college to clarify some point I did not understand. I subsequently made a good grade in the class, where 40% of the students made a D or an F. The professor announced in class, after the final exam, that only two people had taken him up on his offer of assistance. How many were afraid of appearing stupid? This is an example of what psychologists call a "self-fulfilling prophesy".

As you can see, the framework that you learned for evaluating yourself and your experiences has a tremendous influence on how you now direct your life. This framework does not allow room for your emotions and needs. Important mentors exposed you to a way of talking to yourself that ultimately leads to frustration and failure. Now you must confront your judgmental structure, question how you talk to yourself, and brick by brick, command by command, deconstruct your own prison.

The Judgmental Structure

Many people dream of having a perfect mate. Parents often long for perfect children, feeling frustration and guilt when they produce limited and imperfect human beings. The judgmental structure is built upon such expectations and demands. The unrealistic, and indeed impossible, quest for perfection leads to a constant preoccupation with what is lacking. The parent who chides, "You got a 95 on this exam. Why not a 100?" is building a structure of faultfinding, blaming, personal disappointment, resentment and anger.

Connie Evans lives in such a toxic inner environment. Connie is on the fast track as an arbitrage risk analyst in a global hedge fund. She has colleagues, who think nothing of a sixty or seventy hour workweek. Connie is making lots of money, but not having lots of fun. She has almost no social life, travels two to three weeks a month, eats fast food in excess and then fasts to stay in shape. Connie is beginning to realize that her other life goals of having a relationship and a family keep disappearing for weeks at a time under unremitting waves of work.

Connie bargains with her inner self, "I'll take some time once this next project is finished. If I say *no* now, I'll look uninvolved. I need to prove that I'm on the team. There are plenty of people out there who want my job. If I'm not perceived as dedicated, I'll lose out."

In therapy, Connie reports an interesting dream. Her house is filled with strangers. They steal her jewelry and even her canned food. She can't get the strangers out of her house. In this dream Connie tells herself everything she needs to know about her current predicament. Connie has lost her necessary boundaries. She has gone far beyond her internal point of balance. She is losing much of what is precious to her. In her dream, she has written a screenplay of her current psychological state. She is overwhelmed. Her Judge has taken over her life, stealing many precious experiences and robbing her not only of her jewels, but also of her basic means of self-nurture (her food reserves).

If we look at Connie's inner Dialogue, her way of talking to herself, we can see that she is trapping herself with a combination of commands (Drivers), prohibitions (Stoppers), and faulty thinking (Confusers).

Drivers

As the word indicates, a Driver is an internal push. "Get busy! Do it right! Take it like a man! Do something!" Drivers are based upon the Imposed Self notions of what we should do. We are ordered to "Be Perfect, Hurry Up, Please Others, Try Hard, or Be Strong", terms coined by Tabia Kahler. Drivers generate tension. They put you into high gear. To the Judge, a natural pace is not sufficient. You must be better, faster, or stronger.

The term Driver is not synonymous with the psychological concept of drive or motivation. Motivation or drive, like energy or enthusiasm, flows naturally from the Intrinsic Self. A Driver is buoyed up by a kind of forced motivation, a pressure from the Imposed Self that may have no connection at all to a person's inner well of aliveness and energy. A motivated writer may work on a manuscript for eight hours at a stretch, fully enjoying this creative pursuit, wishing to do nothing else. This is far different from the writer whose Judge says, "You should write. You must do it perfectly. Try hard to finish it."

Connie is driven by what analyst Karen Horney once termed the "tyranny of the should." Her Imposed Self tells her, "You must be the best. You must work a fourteen-hour day. You should work on Saturday."

Connie has yet to learn that Drivers demand the impossible. Her day does not have unlimited hours; her energy level is not boundless; her patience is not inexhaustible. However, her Judge believes that all of these things *should* be.

Stoppers

Connie's Judge not only pushes her to act against her feelings and needs, it also blocks her natural expression. These blocks are called Stoppers, which prevent you from doing what your feelings suggest. They discourage any natural spontaneity with harsh judgments, threats, and rigid requirements. Certainly, stopping yourself from acting is sometimes in your own best interest. You learn to stop at a traffic light before crossing the street. You censor harmful actions. However, all too often, the actions that are inhibited and the feelings that are squelched are very important ones, crucial to your own wellbeing.

In Connie's case, Stoppers are seriously interfering with her ability to achieve balance in her life. She allows her boss to call her at all hours over the weekend. She has no down time. She blocks asserting her boundaries with the thought, "I'll seem inadequate." Connie inhibits herself in other ways as well. She almost never takes a vacation, because it isn't "a good time." She cancels dates with friends because she is afraid of being "unprepared" for the next work assignment. Because what she tells herself is totally accepted as fact, Connie has no basis for testing her assumptions. So, she is trapped by her own Stoppers just as surely as if she were confined by another person.

Confusers

Connie constantly scares herself with the thought "I'll lose my job." Setting any boundaries means a frightening foray onto thin ice. This is a Confuser, a way of perceiving and thinking that prevents her from clearly experiencing the world. Connie's evaluation, "I'll lose my job", emerges from an all-or-nothing framework. Connie believes that either she must be one hundred percent perfect, or she has no value. Under this Confuser, she gives herself no credit for what she has done in the past. Connie infers that she is under the gun each and every moment. And because she totally believes her negative inference, she never considers checking it out. Even when other employees seem to manage having a life, Connie clings to her belief that she is holding on to her job by a thread.

From the Judge to your Guide

If Connie were not operating from the Imposed Self position, her relationship with herself would be vastly different. Instead of driving or stopping or confusing her, her inner voice would coach or guide her. She would have as an inner companion someone who cares for her and is concerned with her wellbeing. This inner coach would serve her as a good parent or a supportive friend.

Your response to a stressful situation will depend very much on whether your Imposed Self is functioning as a Judge or a Guide. In many situations the differing reactions can range from a minor feeling of disappointment to total despair. For Bill, not getting an A on a graduate school term paper causes profound feelings of worthlessness. For Jeff, a rejection notice on a grant proposal, on which he has worked for over a year, has little adverse effect.

The difference between each of these two individuals is his self-talk. Bill has a very critical Imposed Self. He judges anything less than an A (even a B) as a failure. Receiving a B easily precipitates in Bill the critique "You failed. It wasn't a good paper. I guess you just don't have it in you. You may not be graduate material. You're not going to be successful. You're a loser." Notice that in his diatribe, Bill does not mention any specific negative consequences that will result from his B grade. His entire focus is on his own critical self-evaluation.

Conversely, when Jeff is not awarded a government grant, he has the following dialogue with himself: " Looks like you didn't get the grant. That really sucks. Oh, well, it means you'll have to start writing another proposal before long. If you had made it this time, it would have saved some work, and that equipment would have come in handy. But that's okay. You can make do. It's no catastrophe."

Jeff stays totally away from self-evaluative judgmental statements. He has a momentary burst of anger, but isn't stuck in it. This is because the approval of his grant is not tied to his self-esteem. While he admits the negative aspects of the rejection, he has no corresponding feelings of worthlessness.

As Epictetus put it thousands of years ago, "Man is troubled not by things, but by the view he takes of them." Thus, situation *A* does not automatically lead to outcome *C*. You have a chance to modify or worsen what happens to you though your self-talk *B*. Simply formatted by Albert Ellis, the grandfather of cognitive therapy, *A+B=C*. The actual situation combines with what you tell yourself to produce feelings and behaviors. Your overall level of stress depends upon how you talk to yourself. The external event, in and of itself, is not the determining factor.

Let's now examine Drivers and their role in your life.

CHAPTER 2

Drivers

Nathaniel Hawthorne's short story "The Birthmark," introduces Aylmer, an eminent man of science, who marries Georgiana, a beautiful woman, flawless in all respects except one. On her lovely face lies a small but clearly perceptible mark. Aylmer is shocked by "this slightest possible imperfection." It becomes unbearable to him, "causing him more trouble and horror than ever Georgiana's beauty…had given him delight." Finding an elixir to remove the flaw, he is ecstatic. For a few moments he beholds perfection. Then as fate would have it, his wife dies from the after-effects of the magic draught.

Long before psychologists documented the detrimental effects of rigid, judgmental standards, writers like Hawthorne knew that ultimate tragedy is born from unrealistic demands and expectations. The story of one man's search for perfection, and its costs, speaks vividly of the push to act in ways that are ultimately harmful. The most pernicious Driver of all, the one of which Hawthorne wrote, is the Driver *Be Perfect*.

Be Perfect

The notion that we ought to *Be Perfect* is pervasive in our society. We forget an appointment and all hell breaks loose inside. "That shouldn't have happened," the Imposed Self castigates. "How can you be so stupid?"

Caught in the grip of *Be Perfect*, we constantly grade ourselves. It is a bizarre Pass/Fail system. One hundred percent perfect and we pass. Anything less and we fail. No matter what the task, *Be Perfect* is present. If we can't do something right, we don't do anything at all.

Being Perfect frequently encompasses other Drivers as well. Based on your own unique learning history, perfection may manifest in terms of accomplishment (the Drivers *Hurry Up* and *Try Hard*). You may see it in becoming a veritable Superman or Superwoman (the Driver *Be Strong*). Or again, perfection may require self-sacrifice (the Driver *Please Others*). For some, all Drivers operate at once. As one group member confessed, "I'm a dentist. I *Try Hard* to *Please Others* so that I can *Be Perfect*."

Jill is a poster girl for the *Be Perfect* structure. Currently, she is in a self-defeating *Be Perfect* conflict around dieting. For the past ten years, she has seesawed between 125 and 155 pounds. Parties are a misery for her. Not only does she dislike the way she looks, but parties also have food, and the temptation to eat is overwhelming. If she eats, she is likely to eat too much. However, if she doesn't eat, she will feel deprived and will make up for her deprivation later when she is at home alone.

Jill is hungry most of the time. Most days are 900-calorie days. She doesn't allow herself pizza or pasta or sweets. She barely eats breakfast or lunch. Yet in spite of her tight rein, Jill views herself as someone who lacks willpower. Along with her nearly constant self-deprivation, she faces a steady stream of self-deprecation as well.

If Jill is so conscientious about her 900-calorie diet, then why doesn't she lose weight? The answer is simple. Jill periodically binges. She comes home and eats anything and everything she can find: a half-gallon of ice cream, a box of cookies, or a loaf of bread. She eats them quickly, without any real enjoyment, and her mounting disgust with herself simply makes her want to eat more. Jill's binges may continue for several hours or several days, during which time she regains all the weight and more that she has lost by her Spartan regimen.

Jill is caught in a diet/binge vise. For her, the decision to diet is a kind of New Year's resolution. It is predicated on perfection. The standard contract reads, "Until I reach 115 pounds, under no circumstances will I ever eat more than 1,000 calories a day, or have starchy, sweet, or otherwise unhealthy food." A casual scrutiny of this resolution reveals its *Be Perfect* premise. Another clause, "If I do not keep this agreement with myself, then I am a failure and a contemptible person," makes it absolute.

Once the resolution is made, Jill is indeed perfect, as far as the diet is concerned, for a day or a week or even for a month. But there will come a time when the she is tired or upset or lonely or just plain too hungry to resist a certain food, and then the *Be Perfect* spell will be broken.

At a low moment, Jill eats a couple of potato chips. For a non-dieter, or someone who isn't controlled by *Be Perfect*, this momentary slip would not be a problem. After all, a few potato chips have at most 50 calories. But to Jill, the weight of the potato chips, is enough to crack the *Be Perfect* structure that she is bound to follow.

With her slip, Jill begins an immediate Imposed Self reproach: "Why did you do that! You're hopeless. You've been doing so well. Why did you have to blow it? You have no self-control." Jill's self-criticism begins to generate negative feelings, primarily anxiety and depression. She has dealt with such feelings in the past by eating, so now she takes a handful of potato chips.

Jill's anxiety is momentarily quelled by eating more, but it soon resounds with greater intensity, and she finds herself caught in the vicious cycle of binge eating. Each new mistake leads to more anxiety and self-punishment, which leads to further eating. A handful of potato chips provokes a tirade against herself that has profound negative repercussions. Jill begins to binge. This *does* lead to weight gain. Even worse, it creates in Jill a sense of hopelessness and self-contempt. That a small deviation from a prescribed plan can have such a major destructive effect demonstrates the power of the *Be Perfect* Driver.

After a number of weeks of therapy, Jill defined her dilemma: "Keeping to my diet is like walking a tightrope. One false move, and I've had it. I can't walk a tightrope forever. I have to let myself walk on a sidewalk. I need to be able to make a mistake occasionally."

Sounds reasonable. Why was it so hard for Jill to recognize that her Drivers prevented rather than helped her lose weight? Like many of us, Jill feared that without her Drivers she would end up lying lazily in the sunshine all day eating bonbons. Worse yet, she would accomplish nothing and life would pass her by. In actuality, however, free of her internal dictates, Jill will accomplish more. She will become easier to live with; her self-respect will increase.

An old saying sums it up: "The *Perfect* is the enemy of the *Good*." By pushing and prodding, Drivers direct you away from a natural pace. Because of their unremitting demands and their blindness to reality, Drivers are detrimental to the very tasks they are supposed to support. Consider the examples candidly shared by members of one group:

"I'm a first child. My father taught me all of the Drivers, particularly *Be Strong*. I push myself to the point that I get sick."

"I ended up with severe depression. I was so busy pleasing other people that I forgot to take care of me."

"I make lists and *Try Hard* to complete them. A little voice says to me, 'Anyone would have done this. Why haven't you gotten it done?' Then I become defiant and don't do anything at all."

"I had to do an oral report in class, and I couldn't eat or sleep in thinking about it. My *Be Perfect* got the best of me. I ended up with a migraine and had to take an incomplete in the class."

The end result of obeying one's Drivers is frequently failure. Invariably, we rebel or collapse in the face of their relentless pressure. We go on a "*Sit-*

Down Strike." This Sit-Down Strike occurs as an alternative to the tightrope. Because we can't do something perfectly, we end up not doing it at all. We turn off, burn out, rebel, or get depressed.

Alcohol and drugs frequently aid in the Sit-Down Strike. Thus Linda comes home from work each night, pours herself a couple of martinis, and collapses on the sofa. She sees no other choice. Without the help of alcohol, she would worry about today's mistakes and plan for tomorrow's crises all evening. By the end of an already stressful day, she is only too happy to have this martini-induced option of rest and relaxation. The only problem is that she must knock herself out. She has learned no other means of turning off her *Be Perfect, Hurry Up*, and *Try Hard* demands.

Linda lacks an alternative to both the pressure of the Driver and the indulgence of the Sit-Down Strike. She needs to create inner affirmations and supports for her Intrinsic Self. These are referred to as Permitters. They allow room for flexibility. They loosen the grip of internal commands. They allow one to ease off the tightrope onto a sidewalk. Moreover, unlike the rebellious, defiant, or exhausted reaction of the Sit-Down Strike, Permitters allow us to proceed forward. Knowing "It's okay to be human; it's okay to make mistakes; and it's okay to take my time" leads to feelings and behaviors far different from the "I'll do nothing" decision of the Sit-Down Strike.

Hurry Up

The second Driver, *Hurry Up*, pushes us to do things quickly. It commands, "Do more and more in less and less time".

Trapped in the *Hurry Up* vise, Marvin is frequently impatient and angry. Continually playing "Beat the Clock", he describes the experience like this: "My watch is constantly burning a hole in my wrist. There's never time to do what I want. I scold myself constantly. I push the kids the same way: 'Hurry up and make your beds. Hurry up and eat your cereal.' I have no space in my life, no breathing room."

Hurry Up is one of the easiest Drivers to identify. A sure test is to observe how you drive. Are you annoyed when a car in front of you pauses for an extra seconds when the light turns green? Do you weave in and out of traffic to get someplace five minutes sooner? Are you quick to use the horn? If you answer *yes*, you can claim to have a *Hurry Up* Driver.

Hurry Up pushes around other people as well. I once told a class that I would give them five minutes to write their self-dialogues if they arrived late for a meeting. In giving the class only five minutes to do a fairly complex exercise, it's likely that my own *Hurry Up* Driver was in force. But there was also a *Hurry Up* in at least one class member. With seeming annoyance, Nell asserted, "We don't need that long!"

The book *Type A Behavior and Your Heart* recognized the *Hurry Up* Driver as a major component of Type A Behavior. Reflecting a constant sense of time urgency, impatience, and an excessive competitive drive, Type A Behavior has been associated with coronary heart disease. Authors Friedman and Rosenman state, "Overwhelmingly, the most significant trait of the Type A (person) is his habitual sense of time urgency or *hurry sickness*." This internal pressure, characterized by the command, "Full steam ahead", causes a person to react with anger and irritation, predisposing them to the increased risk of heart attacks.

Society rewards those who "*Hurry Up*". Setting short deadlines meets with promotions and acclaim. The cost of the overwork is frequently not experienced until later, when friends, family, and important parts of one's own self have been discarded and left far behind. The irony is that the colleagues you sacrificed so much to please make themselves notable by their absence when you are recovering from a stress related illness or have an automobile accident from rushing about while preoccupied by a work-related crisis.

The great naturalist John Muir is said to have "viewed with sadness" the distinguished visitors who came to Yosemite, calling them "time poor." According to Muir's biographer, Edwin Way Teale, he "chose to be *time rich* first of all". Muir wrote to his sister, "I have not yet in all my wanderings found a single person so free as myself. When in the woods, I sit at times for hours watching birds and squirrels or looking down into the faces of flowers without suffering any feelings of haste." Could you ever say the same? For that matter, how many of us allow even thirty minutes each day to contemplate the beauty of nature, or to allow our thoughts to drift?

Simply deciding to take some time off or to relax each day has little effect unless you also change what you say to yourself. I can recall once going through a relaxation exercise all the while thinking of what I had to hurry up and do when I finished. "Why is this tape taking so long?" my train of thought went. I was actually worse off physiologically after my "relaxation", than before I started.

The Permitter opposing *Hurry Up* states, "It's okay to relax and take my time. Everything does not have to be accomplished today or even tomorrow." Those of you, who think that you cannot possibly give yourself this permission, may wish to consider Friedman and Rosenman's warning: "You are only finished when you're dead."

Perhaps here is a good place to counter the objection, "But I can't take my time. I work in a crucial position. I have to hurry." This objection rests upon a misunderstanding of what Permission actually involves. Let me illustrate. I once helped a nurse to lower her anxiety in the operating room. Here, of all places, speed is of the essence. However, hounding herself with *Hurry Up* did not help. Here as everywhere else, pushing past her capacity meant making errors.

The Permission "It's okay to take the time I need to respond accurately" was very effective in lowering her anxiety during a difficult operation. Far from hindering her effectiveness in the operating room, this Permission greatly enhanced it. And, she stopped dropping things.

Be Strong

The *Be Strong* Driver argues that certain feelings are unacceptable, even despicable. Any need is a weakness to be overcome. Feelings of sadness, hurt, or loneliness are intolerable. According to the *Be Strong* command, you should be able to handle *on your own* all the problems that come your way.

Because the *Be Strong* Driver says, "You must do it all yourself," those who need help are unable to ask for it. *Be Strong* individuals despise themselves for having needs or feelings and may view psychotherapy with contempt. Not infrequently, someone in my office will start crying and then immediately begin a tirade, "I don't know why I'm doing this. This is so stupid." Some people go even further to stop their "weak" reactions. They clench their fists or bite their lips, because the expression of sadness is experienced as a humiliation.

As with all Drivers, the *Be Strong* command represents an accepted, even admired, way of behaving in our society. This is particularly true for men. The strong, silent movie hero exemplifies society's ideal of the self-reliant individual who knows how "to take things like a man," that is, without visible emotion or feeling. Even the experience of pain is supposed to be borne as stoically as possible. Of course, *Be Strong* can shape the behavior of women as well. One of my female clients was so affected by the *Be Strong* Driver that she did not allow herself to ask for a local anesthetic during a painful operation, in which she had a mole removed. She would have faced severe self-reproach if she had expressed this need to her doctor.

The *Be Strong* Driver develops under circumstances where important others are severely critical of softness or vulnerability. A parent threatens, "If you don't stop crying, I'll give you something to cry about!" Having been ridiculed or punished when sadness or sensitive feelings emerged, children begin to treat themselves in the same manner.

The blunting of one child's sensitivity and compassion can be seen from an experience recalled by Lyndon Johnson in Doris Kearns's biography *Lyndon Johnson and the American Dream:*

"In the fall and the spring, I spent every moment when I wasn't in school out in the open. With other boys, I went hunting squirrels and rabbits. I carried a gun, and every now and then I pointed it at the animals, but I never wanted to kill any of them. I wanted only to know that I could kill if I had to. Then one day my daddy asked me how did it happen that I was the only boy in the neighborhood who had never shot an animal. Was I a coward? The next day I went back into the hills and killed a rabbit. It jumped out at me from behind a bush, and I shot it between the eyes. Then I went into the bathroom and threw up."

Years later, Johnson gave male visitors to the LBJ Ranch rifles and cajoled them to shoot a deer or an antelope in his presence. According to Kearns, Johnson was putting his visitors' manhood to the test, as his father had once challenged his own.

The Permission, "It's okay to have feelings and to express them" opposes the *Be Strong* Driver. Hurt feelings, sad feelings, tender feelings, vulnerable feelings, and needy feelings are all acceptable. Permission to express these feelings with others is equally important. Allowing oneself to cry alone is not the same as expressing sadness to another person.

Please Others

The Driver *Please Others* says that we are okay only when other people like and approve of us. Losing this approval even for a moment can lead to high levels of anxiety and depression. If you operate from a *Please Others* Driver, you will have a difficult time asserting your own needs and feelings, such as saying *no* to requests and demands from friends or relatives. You may even inhabit the position of Charles, a man in one of my first groups, who confessed, " I have spent my entire life doing what other people wanted me to do. Now, I don't even know who I am, and my despair seems overwhelming."

Unplugging the *Please Others* Driver will not prevent the give-and-take inherent in any good relationship. Pleasing another person is enjoyable and rewarding. However, many people please others at great personal expense. While developing an exquisite sensitivity to the nuances of the emotional state of other people, they remain oblivious to their own. A woman caught in the *Please Others* Driver fails to recognize her own anger and resentment until long after a provocative incident has occurred. Not surprisingly, sociologist Suzanne Keller tells us that a basic tenet of the traditional feminine role is the command that "women should live through and for others", a direct injunction to *Please Others*.

Like many women, Norma yoked her life to the requirements of someone else. "When George was home," Norma shared, "I was always on the lookout for anything that might trigger his anger. I went around paving the way for him, making sure the kids weren't too noisy, stepping in to locate something he couldn't find, doing anything to keep him calm. I was his valet in almost every sense of that word. Even when I was visiting someone, I would base my departure on the mood I determined he would be in when I got home. I never considered my own feelings at all. I spent nine years of marriage monitoring his!"

"It's okay to please myself" is the Permitter that Norma lacked. Pleasing herself meant considering her own feelings and needs. It meant allowing herself to pursue her own unique agenda. It did not mean that she would never choose to please another, but as a choice, one that consciously took her own feelings into consideration. The *Please Others* Driver gave her no choice. One step off the tightrope meant a disastrous fall into self-loathing.

Try Hard

The fifth Driver, *Try Hard*, was initially the most difficult for me to understand. The reason for my blind spot was simple. *Try Hard* is my favorite Driver. Involving the push to take on more and more, *Try Hard* is impervious to setting appropriate limits.

I recently had a chance to change a negative situation involving my own *Try Hard* Driver. Having subscribed to a local newspaper, I pushed myself to read it each day and to tear out certain articles. If I was tired after work, I stacked the paper in the corner, with the resolution that I would *Try Hard* to look it over the next day. Usually, I faced the weekend with a stack of newspapers that I nagged myself to read, while my house grew increasingly cluttered with clippings.

Finally, I gave myself permission to let go. I stopped buying the newspaper, to the great benefit of both my home and my sanity. The honest truth of the matter was that I didn't really want to read the paper. I only felt that I should. This is the crux of the Driver *Try Hard*. It pushes us to accept a burden without concern for our wishes or for our emotional and physical limits.

The *Try Hard* Driver is inevitably present when we are caught in a "Rescue Operation." I was first introduced to the rescue concept by family therapist and author, Shirley Luthman. When we rescue someone, we take responsibility for that person and for his problems. Helping professionals (psychologists, physicians, nurses, police officers, and others) are particularly vulnerable to the *Try Hard* Driver. Placed in situations where their jobs involve helping people in need, they often ignore their own personal limits. The ultimate consequence is "Burn Out". Dr. Christina Maslach, in an article in *Human Behavior,* states, "After hours, days, and months of listening to other people's problems, something inside of you can go dead, and you don't give a damn anymore."

Jenny found herself feeling this way toward her friend Martha. She loaned Martha money and put her own grades in jeopardy when she helped Martha complete a report. Having gone to such trouble for her, Jenny couldn't understand why Martha seldom called or wanted to get together.

In helping Martha solve her problems, Jenny forgot to consider her own limits. Now she feels resentful, and Martha feels guilty. Jenny would have fared better if she had supported Martha *and* been sensitive to her own boundaries. This balance can be achieved only by steering clear of Drivers like *Try Hard*, which leave no room for one's own feelings and needs.

Opposing *Try Hard* are the Permissions "It's okay to say *no*" and "It's okay to let go." In other words, you can choose *not* to try hard. You can decide not to participate on five committees, or even on one committee, if you do not want to participate. You can decide not to *Try Hard* to spend time with a new acquaintance or to take on another project, no matter how worthy. In short, you can recognize your own limits, in work, in friendship, and in intimate relationships. Further, with Permissions like, "It's okay to ask for the support I need to meet my goal; It's okay to acknowledge the real difficulties inherent in my project; and It's okay to set limits in other areas," you no longer will need to *Try Hard*. You can simply meet your commitments to yourself.

Driver-Related Costs

The paradoxical result of obeying your Drivers is the very lack of accomplishment, the vulnerability, and the interpersonal difficulties, which you wanted to avoid by honoring them in the first place. Drivers take you along a pernicious and far-ranging course. You will see their costs reflected in your behaviors, your feelings, your level of stress, your interpersonal relationships, and your self-esteem. Thus Aileen, whose *Hurry Up* Driver blares all day at work, comes home at night after work, goes to bed at seven, and sleeps until the next morning. She ignores her internal signals of fatigue and tension at work, and when her shift ends, she is wiped out.

Aileen's exhaustion has certain consequences, one of which is the curtailment of social activities, a vital ingredient of her wellbeing. She ends up depleted and empty. What Aileen does to replace this emptiness is to drink. Also, she loads up on fast, fattening foods on her way home from work, knowing that she will be too tired to cook. She gains weight, and when she finds that her clothes no longer fit, her self-esteem drops. She loses energy and enthusiasm for her job.

We could develop this downward spiral even further. But, let's assume that Aileen recognizes that she is getting into trouble and consults a therapist. To the therapist she may say, "I have a weight problem" or "I don't feel very good about myself." It would be unlikely for her to have the insight to consider, "I drive myself too hard at work." Yet that is her problem. Her other difficulties are simply consequences of the Drivers *Hurry Up* and *Try Hard.*

If Aileen were to look closely, she would realize that there are relatively few times during her day when she actually has to rush. Her usual *Hurry Up* behavior (reading while she eats lunch, walking rapidly from one place to another, skipping breaks, growing impatient with conversation, returning messages at once) rests upon her internal push. If she calculated the costs, she might consider disengaging.

So it is with other Drivers. Their promised glory fails to materialize. The *Be Perfect* writer, whose critic sits frowning on her shoulder, suffers writer's block. The single woman looking for the perfect mate ends up having no one. The *Please Others* husband or wife becomes a resentful martyr. The *Be Strong* loner commits suicide. The *Try Harder* volunteer burns out, and replaces her admirable intentions with cynicism.

The picture that I am painting is, of course, extreme. For most people, Drivers only hinder creativity. They simply generate bad feelings, and merely interfere with interpersonal relationships. For most of us, Drivers do not destroy completely the push toward growth. Yet the demands of the tightrope are severe. Any fall can lead to a sense of failure, to depression, and to a loss of self-esteem. The glittering coin whose face offers the chance to grasp an image of perfection hides on its underside both despair and self-hate. Pick up the coin, and you inevitably embrace both.

Your Driver Profile

One way to understand you own Drivers is to examine the influences from your past. Psychologist Portia Shapiro developed an exercise on Influence Analysis to help you do this. First, draw a circle in the center of a piece of paper. This circle in the center represents you. Next, around this circle, draw five other circles, each one representing an important person in your life. The people you chose may be living or dead. You may not even know some of them on a person-to-person level. The circles may describe a group of people (my senior class) or an organization (the Catholic Church). If a book character, a public figure, or a movie star had an important influence in your life, acknowledge that reality here. When each circle is drawn and labeled, list specifically any Drivers (*Be Perfect, Hurry Up, Try Hard, Please Others,* or *Be*

Strong) that you incorporated from this significant person or group. Now go back and note the Permitters that you acquired from these past influences.

By recognizing the origins of your own Drivers, you gain a greater distance from them. The toxic process, which upholds the judgmental position, loosens its hold on you. The choice becomes yours. You can continue driving yourself, or you can develop new Permissions on which to base your inner speech.

CHAPTER 3

Stoppers

If I have an idea," Sheila began, "I first say to myself, 'What I'm thinking is probably not that important or someone else would have already said it'. Then, if someone does express my idea, I tell myself, 'You were an idiot not to have spoken up!' I really can't win with myself. Even describing this right now makes me think, 'How silly!'"

Do you, like Sheila, interfere with your own spontaneous self-expression, thus confining yourself to a limited life? Do you inhibit the natural unfolding of your actions and feelings? If so, you are familiar with Stoppers, those internal self-messages that say "*No*", "*Don't*", and "*Only if*".

Stoppers were the first form of self-talk that caught my attention. I began noticing the effects of Stoppers in my assertiveness training workshops. I found that a negative judgment, a confining rule, or an anxious concern stopped people from expressing themselves. A man doesn't approach a woman (or vice versa) to ask out on a date for fear of appearing "on the make". A woman can't say "no" to working late because she tells herself, "It won't kill me." An honest difference of opinion is avoided because one party concludes, "I should be above this."

Fritz Perls, founder of modern Gestalt Therapy, once said, "Man is the only organism who interferes with his own growth." Think for a moment what this means. Think of the inner messages by which you prevent yourself from pursuing interests or contacts that would make your life more exciting and you a better person. Think of the self-rejection that occurs in the form of, "You couldn't be a writer/artist/engineer/ or business owner. You're too young/old/ignorant/ or untalented." Or the self-talk that keeps you from pursuing opportunities, "He won't remember you. Don't bother to call back." When we examine the painful comparisons that people make about themselves, about their appearances, their children, or their levels of success, we can surely note that these Stoppers do not help. In fact, they create feelings of hopelessness and despair. In contrast, imagine an oak tree being depressed because the dogwood tree beside it has blooms, and it doesn't. Or, think of a cheetah on the African savanna being self conscious of how it might look chasing a gazelle.

The term Stopper was originally applied by psychiatrist Eric Berne to negative messages like "Don't be," "Don't grow up," or "Don't be normal." I have expanded the Stopper concept to include Catastrophizing, Negative Self-Labeling, and Setting Rigid Requirements.

Before describing each Stopper process, let's examine a situation that we'll call "stranger across a crowded room", in which all of them tend to occur. Imagine yourself at a social gathering where you don't know anyone. Perhaps it's the social hour after a professional conference. Perhaps it's a "Drop by, we're having some friends over" invitation from a casual acquaintance. Whichever situation it is, you are with a group of strangers, thinking, "What do I do now?"

After allowing yourself time to get your bearings, you look around and spot someone across the room you think you might like to meet. Perhaps this person looks particularly interesting or attractive to you. Or you notice an individual who offered some controversial comments at your conference workshop. Whatever the source of your interest, if you are not talking to yourself in a negative manner (i.e. if your Imposed Self is functioning as a Guide rather than as a Judge), chances are that you will walk up to the person, introduce yourself, and make an opening comment. Even if you have some initial reluctance to do this, your action will be supported with statements to yourself like "Hey, what can you lose? This is a social gathering. You're here to talk. I bet that person over there would enjoy meeting you. Go ahead," or "That's the woman who made those interesting observations. I bet that she'd like to know how someone reacted to her comments. If not, that's okay, but give it a try."

On the other hand, if you are listening to your Judge, you will probably not act. Your original impulse to extend yourself will be dampened by your inner dialogue. "Ah," you begin, "there's the woman I've been wanting to meet. I think I'll go over and introduce myself." Fine so far. Only notice now how Stoppers begin to surface. "Wait a minute," your Judge commences. "Just because you want to meet her, doesn't mean that she wants to meet you. What if you walk over, and she sees you coming and turns away? That would be awful. And even if she's interested in meeting you, how can you be sure that you won't be boring? What have you got to say that's all that important? I know! If she looks in your direction and smiles, then walk over. See? She's just smiled. Wait a minute. How do you know she was smiling at you? If she smiles again, go…"

In relating this Stopper dialogue to groups, I usually exaggerate toward the end to help people see the "no risk" wall that they are carefully constructing around themselves. Of course, a person carrying on this kind of self-dialogue will rarely make it across a room (or even make it two or three feet for that matter) to converse with another person. Such self-dialogue results in self-rejection. Can you determine the number of Stoppers in this brief inner conversation? There are six. Two are examples of *Catastrophizing*, two are *Negative Self-Labeling*, and two are *Rigid Requirements*. Let's examine in detail each of these Stopper processes.

Catastrophizing

Catastrophizing, a term first coined by psychologist Albert Ellis, is the internal rehearsal of all the horrible, catastrophic events that might possibly occur if you were to engage in a particular behavior.

Catastrophizing interferes with the realistic solution to the equation "Action equals Benefit-to-be-Obtained over Risk-to-be-Taken." When you Catastrophize, you exaggerate the risk factor so much that you decide to do nothing. In our imagined party scene, the Judge catastrophizes that the woman across the room would not want to become acquainted. ("Just because you want to meet her, doesn't mean she wants to meet you.") Because this improbable scenario was considered "awful" in its eventuality, the opportunity to act upon the desires of the Intrinsic Self was rejected.

The key phrases in Catastrophizing are "What if?" and "That would be awful." The phrase "So what if" is one neutralizer. As you become more growth-oriented, you will find that most "That would be awful" self-talk does not focus on the realistic consequences of an action but on the self-evaluative ones. In other words, most times you would suffer little external harm if your Catastrophes actually occurred. Thus, when someone Catastrophizes, "It would be awful if I asked for a raise and didn't get it," the "awful" relates to feelings of embarrassment or injured pride at being turned down. The realistic consequence of not getting the raise is often, paradoxically, an increased chance of getting one the next time.

If you find yourself blocked by fears and catastrophes, try writing down each one as a "What if" statement. Some examples are: "What if Geoff doesn't ask me out again?" "What if my presentation isn't well received?" or "What if I try out for a part in the play and don't get it?" Next, determine if your own "What if…" fear involves a realistic consequence or a self-evaluative one. In other words, does not getting the part in a play lead more to a genuine loss or to bad feelings about yourself? Self-evaluative consequences can be drastically reduced as you alter your own self-talk. Examine the Catastrophes listed below. Do any of these "What if…" fears inhibit you? What if…

I make a mistake?
I can't find a perfect solution?
Someone doesn't want to see me again?
I'm wrong?
My opinion is challenged?
Someone gets angry with me?
I'm disapproved of?
I get angry?
I get emotional?
I lose my job?
My relationship doesn't work out?
I'm criticized?
I can't think of anything to say?
I am rejected?
I blush?
My voice is shaky?
Everyone doesn't consider me to be a nice person?
Someone doesn't listen to me?
Someone knows more than I do?

Now, in front of each statement, try "so what if…." Note the difference in your feelings. Would it really be so awful if one of these events occurred? Think about it. The answer may surprise you.

Negative Self-Labeling

Negative Self-Labeling involves attaching negative judgments to natural and healthy impulses of the Intrinsic Self. Labels like "boring" and "not that important" make it difficult to act on signals from the Intrinsic Self. These labels come from the Judge, whose critical eye is always ready to punish and ridicule a push toward growth.

The impulse to be assertive is very vulnerable to the effect of Negative Self-Labeling. Each of the four areas of assertive expression is associated with a plethora of such labels. If you want to express positive feelings toward someone, you caution yourself against sounding "insincere" or "gushy." If you have an impulse to say something positive about yourself, labels like "conceited" and "bragging" frighten you into silence. Your assertion of negative feelings is squashed by concerns about "nagging" or "being mean". Setting limits, or saying "No", elicits the guilt inducing epitaphs, "selfish" or "unfeeling". When you tell yourself that what you want to say or do is "unimportant" or "dumb", you squash self-initiation and creativity.

Listen to Millie, "I spent three hours writing three sentences. Every word I wrote, I labeled: 'That sounds funny.' 'That doesn't make the point.' 'That word is outdated.' 'Don't sound so cute.' I was soon so disgusted with myself and my paper that I just decided to go to sleep."

I hear examples like Millie's over and over. The Judge punishes us with negative labels to the point that all the fun is taken out of our lives. Contrast Millie's description with that of author Llewelyn Powys, who describes in *The Creative Process* how he ignores any negative labels. Powys writes, "My own method is to give no thought whatever to the form of what I am writing. I put down my ideas as they present themselves pell-mell in my mind, fanciful, sentimental, bawdy, irreverent, or irrelevant. They are all equally welcome. In going over my work, however, I am prepared to spend a great deal of care in endeavoring to find the just-right word or an adequate balance for any particular paragraph."

Powys's "critic," as he explains, comes to the fore only after his material has had unhindered access to his paper. No Stoppers interfere with his flow of words. Powys goes on to state, "I consider the greatest difficulty to be overcome by immature, untrained writers is lack of confidence. They are all too self-conscious. When once the pen is in the hand, it is important to forget about the opinions of others and to write away after your own fashion with careless, proud indifference."

Stopper-produced inhibition can occur with sports and leisure activities as well as with creative pursuits. For example, John refused to take up tennis or bridge or skiing because he could not tolerate the self-punishment evoked by being a beginner. He was terrified that his efforts would be seen as inept or stupid. Here again comes self-rejection. Having such a critical view, John found that it is safer to confine himself to those few activities that he had already mastered.

Even when John was willing to try something new, he found his negative Self-Labels interfering with his performance by generating tension. This caused him to avoid the activity in the future. Of course, John was deprived of the joy of learning and eventually mastering a new sport. Negative labels are invariably harsh self-judgments on behaviors that can be interpreted in a different manner. The labels "stupid," "a klutz," or "inept" can be replaced by the label "beginner," one that is much less negative and actually more accurate.

Most negative labels are not based on truth or honesty or on a willingness to see reality but on a harsh, critical stance, which you have learned to apply to yourself. The labels you choose derive from those the significant others in your past once used. If your mentors had strong standards of perfection, and were harsh and critical, your beginning athletic attempts were called "clumsy" instead of appraised as a "good start." After all, it's easy to criticize another person, especially a child. You must continually reevaluate your labels and limit their destructive effects. A good motto to remember in this regard is President Harry Truman's comment, "Any jackass can kick down a barn, but it takes a carpenter to build one." Think of your Intrinsic Self as the carpenter and your Judge as the jackass.

In evaluating your negative labels, it is also important to consider the motives behind any action. For example, your motive in voicing negative feelings may not be to nag or to be mean, but simply to clear the air in order to avoid the buildup of resentment. Similarly, your motive behind playing tennis may not be to rival Steffi Graf, but to get some exercise in an enjoyable format. Beginners probably get more of that anyway, so what does it matter that your game has some distance to go?

Many of these Negative Self Labels may be familiar to you: Nagging, Cold, Compulsive, Dull, Uninteresting, Aggressive, Castrating, Immature, Egotistical, Ungrateful, Irresponsible, Unfeminine, Harsh, Bossy, Parental, Domineering, Selfish, Wrong, Demanding, Illogical, Irrational, Thoughtless, Hysterical, Crazy, Insensitive, Pushy, Impolite, Bitchy, Stupid, Dumb, Shrill, Sissy, Weak, Ugly, Nosy, Incapable, Competitive, Un-masculine, Adamant, Unladylike, Too-much, Soft, Overactive, Troublemaker, Childish, Willful, Self-pitying, Silly, Stuck up, Unimportant, Too-idealistic, Petty, Frigid, Nit-picking, Self-centered, Overly emotional.

Setting Rigid Requirements

Setting Rigid Requirements is the third Stopper process that occurred in the hypothetical situation of seeing someone you want to approach across a crowded room. The statement "I'll walk across the room and approach the woman I would like to meet, *if* she looks in my direction and smiles" is a Rigid Requirement. So is the "*If* she smiles again" addition. Notice the small word *if*. With this one word, a set of conditions is prescribed that must be met before an action can take place. These conditions narrow your choices, blocking feelings and actions. The old adage, "*If* you can't say something nice, don't say anything at all" is a common rigid requirement, one that totally shuts off the expression of negative emotions.

Below, a number of Rigid Requirements are listed. Are any of these in your Stopper repertoire?

I'll follow my feelings, only...

if it is vital,
if someone is not in a bad mood,
if I cannot live with the situation as it stands,
if no one else is around to see me,
if I can't get my spouse to do it,
if the other person will be assertive back,
if I have all the facts or information,
if I have done everything else perfectly,
if the other person can take it,
if I am feeling good about myself,
if it's what I should feel,
if I am sure about what I feel,
if I am justified,
if I am dealing with a peer,
if I won't hurt anyone's feelings,
if I will still be liked,
if no one will be angry with me,
if my assertion is without flaw,
if I can be unobtrusive,
if I'm perfect,
if it's part of my job,
if it's a matter of principle,
if I know the outcome,
if the time is right,
if I don't antagonize,
if it's really going to bug me,
if I can be witty, eloquent, and brilliant.

Rigid Requirements frequently stop behaviors that do not fit the Judge's ideas of what should be. Thus, a person who has learned to follow the Driver *Be Strong* will often have the corresponding requirement "I'll express myself *if* I can do so without being emotional." When followed, this requirement limits the expression of anything of real importance. A person who's Judge says *Please Others* tends to have the Rigid Requirement "I'll speak up *if* I'm sure that I won't hurt anyone's feelings." Since not hurting someone else's feelings is only partly within our control, this requirement blocks the assertion of all limits and negative feelings. A Rigid Requirement obliterating the expression of the Intrinsic Self will be familiar to those with the Drivers *Hurry Up* and *Try Hard*. It goes something like this: "Okay, *if* you finish cleaning the house and sort out your income tax receipts, and complete your ten paged list of "other chores", *then* you can relax." Signals of exhaustion from the Intrinsic Self are not acted upon until these requirements are met.

The antidote to the Rigid Requirement, *if*, is the Permitter, *even if*. Rather than say to myself, "I'll ask a question *if* it's really important," I can say to myself, "I'll ask my question *even if* it is *not* important." To the requirement "I'll speak up *if* I'm sure I won't hurt anyone's feelings," I can state, "I'll speak up *even if* I hurt someone's feelings." If my intent is positive, speaking up is the best course. If I don't express myself now, my feelings will come out later in a destructive way. Many friendships and marriages are destroyed because resentment was allowed to accumulate behind this requirement of not hurting the other's feelings. Eventually, the resentment grows too large to contain and this rigid requirement is pushed aside. Tragically, it is often too late to work out problems that could have been dealt with early on.

Stopper-Related Costs

Because Stoppers interfere with the growth and development of the Intrinsic Self, their cost to heath, happiness and general well-being are extreme. Stoppers exert their negative effects by curtailing spontaneous self-expression. Stoppers confine a person to a narrow, predictable path. One common focus is on time spent on non-work pursuits. Following this path traps a person in the nagging labels of the Judge. Because of Stoppers saying "no" to the small bursts of excitement and interest that fuel our life's meaning, over time, life becomes a routine of get up, go to work, come home, have a drink, watch television, and go to bed. Weekends are for recuperation from the past week and preparation for the next. The Stoppers like, "No Time," "Too Expensive", Too Silly", "Too Old" presage the gradual elimination of adventure and enjoyable activities. A high cost is paid for this self-deprivation.

An individual's feelings signal the first indication of this price. These feelings may hide in words like "Life is not as exciting as it once was" or "My marriage has lost its romance" or "I've burnt out with my job." The tight Stopper reins have produced a stagnation of the Intrinsic Self. Over time, feelings of boredom and ennui may deepen into depression. As vital ingredients of emotional nourishment are discarded, a person's world shrinks into a narrow, unrewarding place. Depression is the Intrinsic Self's signal that too much has been eliminated.

Similarly, depression and other negative emotions occur when Stopper processes block self-assertion. The failure to assert negative feelings, for example, leads to "gunnysacking", the buildup of resentment toward other people. Gunnysacking produces periodic explosions, or the subtle, but equally harmful, process of withdrawal. Both of these reactions strain, and often destroy, interpersonal relationships.

When Stoppers block out interpersonal self-expression, the end result is the shy individual, blocked by anxiety producing self-talk, who cannot reach out to other people. Having once been considered shy myself, I know that shyness doesn't necessarily result from an absence of thoughts but from an absence of thoughts considered acceptable to express.

The self-imposed inhibition, which is shyness, leads to isolation from others and feeds a person's low self-esteem. Tom, for example, has great difficulty engaging in small talk. He labels his ideas as "commonplace," "already known," and "uninteresting," thus stopping himself from sharing just the kind of information that makes up beginning conversations. His Rigid Requirement "I'll speak up *if* I can think of something new to say" results in all too many missed opportunities. His Catastrophe "It would be awful if I said something awkward" makes spontaneous interaction impossible. Because these Stoppers so effectively stifle Tom's communication, he appears to be uninterested in other people. Some people even see him as aloof. What Tom fears most usually happens. He is ignored and left out by others. The tragedy is that this rejection occurs only because Tom has already rejected himself.

Your Stopper Profile

To determine your Stopper profile, you can repeat the exercise that you completed previously with regard to your Drivers. Again, draw a circle in the center of a piece of paper. This circle represents you. Around this center circle, draw five other circles, representing the important people or groups in your life. When each circle is drawn and labeled, write inside it any Catastrophes ("What will the neighbors think"), Negative Labels ("You're selfish"), or Rigid Requirements ("Good people don't get angry"), which you learned from your interactions with these significant others. Also write any permissive messages that were offered to you. These would include messages like "Be yourself" or "Children should be seen and heard" or "To your own self be true." Knowing where your negative messages come from gives you an increased ability to deal with them later.

In the chapters that follow, we will examine how to remove these Stoppers from our paths. Before we do, however, there is one further form of negative self-talk at the disposal of the Judge. The next chapter will introduce us to Confusers.

CHAPTER 4

Confusers

Because we confront a constant barrage of information each day, we develop shorthand to simplify what we perceive. We sort events and people into categories—right or wrong, good or bad. "Either this is true, or that is true," we tell ourselves, while leaving out the entire middle ground. We magnify some experiences, while ignoring others. The benefit of this shorthand is that we simplify our environments. However, we risk venturing away from reality. By necessity, we ignore important factors and misperceive others. Robert Pirsig, the author of *Zen and the Art of Motorcycle Maintenance,* puts it more eloquently: "We take a handful of sand from the endless landscape of awareness around us and call that handful of sand the world."

Aaron Beck, a psychiatrist, who has done pioneering research into the causes and treatments of depression, described five ways of perceiving that distort everyday experience. I call these processes Confusers, because they selectively bias your day-to-day experiences. I have added three to Beck's list, making eight. They are:

1. Arbitrary Inferences
2. Misattribution
3. Cognitive Deficiency
4. Overgeneralization
5. Either/Or Thinking
6. Vague Language
7. Magnification
8. Discounting

Arbitrary Inferences

In one episode of the television show, "The Odd Couple", Felix Unger tells Oscar Madison, "When you *assume*, you make an **ass** out of **u** and **me**." Assumptions are the Arbitrary Inferences that you draw, without careful consideration of the facts involved. If Jim makes the statement, "Mark doesn't like me," Jim assumes that he is stating a fact. Yet this information may not have come from Mark's saying to Jim in a serious manner, "I don't like you." Instead, Jim may have decided this, after putting together the evidence, "Mark hasn't called lately," and "Mark didn't want to play golf the last time I asked." Thus the statement "Mark doesn't like me" is not really a fact. It is an inference. It is a conclusion drawn on the basis of other events, such as Mark's lack of recent contact. In actuality, Mark's feelings toward Jim may not have altered at all. Mark may have good reason for his unavailability.

According to general semanticist Harry Weinberg, the author of *Levels of Knowing and Existence,* a factual statement is "one which is made only after observation and which is verifiable by accepted standards." On the other hand, an inferential statement is one that goes beyond observation to draw a conclusion. Even Jim's evidence for his conclusion has not been distilled to the factual level. The statements "Mark hasn't called lately" and "Mark didn't want to play golf the last time I asked" are also inferences. Jim can consider his first statement to be a fact only if he has an answering service that always works or if he has been at home every moment, his line has never been busy, and there have been no problems along the phone cable. If he is not certain of these factors, his assertion must be "I have not connected with Mark, although he may have tried to call." The same careful scrutiny must occur with his second statement, if Jim wishes to assume that it indeed has a factual base.

Like Jim, you may ignore this very important distinction between facts and inferences. Yet when dealing with inferences, there is always the chance that what you are stating or believing is not true. You cannot count on inferences in the same way that you can rely on facts. Weinberg gives a dramatic example of this discrepancy when he notes how many presumably "unloaded" guns kill people every year. The inference is that the gun is unloaded. The fact is that it was not.

Making inferences in and of itself is not a negative process. After all, an inference is simply a hypothesis to be tested. The problem occurs if you draw conclusions in an arbitrary fashion, without sufficient supporting evidence, or if you fail to recognize that your conclusions may be incorrect. When your inferences relate to your basic opinions about yourself and other people, you too are playing with a loaded gun. Here your inferences have the capacity to do great harm.

In my own experience as a therapist, I see a tremendous amount of psychological pain based on this habit. Inferences like "I'll never meet anyone" or "I can't support myself alone" or "I'll never be happy again" are blatantly false. I see them proved untrue time and time again as I work with someone in therapy. Yet when they are accepted as true and acted upon, they produce destructive consequences.

Inferences typically have more to do with a person's basic belief system than with the actual facts involved in a particular situation. As a result, the same exact circumstance can lead to a variety of inferences. The critical factor is the basic belief of the person drawing the conclusion.

To illustrate this process in a vivid way, I asked one class to respond to the following situation: "Mary sees her friend Paul on the street. She waves, but Paul appears to ignore her. Mary responds. What is her response?" The class gave a variety of answers. Each response related to the inference that the class member had Mary make about Paul.

"If Mary said to herself, 'Oh, no. Paul must not like me anymore. He's ignoring me on purpose,' she'd be depressed," one member began.

Another quickly proposed, "On the other hand, she might think to herself, 'Wow, Paul doesn't recognize me. My new haircut must make me look great.' Then she might feel excited."

A third member offered, "What about her thinking, 'I can't wait to tell Paul that he walked right past me without speaking. I can tease him about that for the next three weeks.'"

A fourth alternative: "She could generate anger if she thought, 'How dare Paul not speak to me! He's a conceited boor. Who does he think he is!'"

Perhaps the best response of all came with the last suggestion: "If Mary says to herself, 'I wonder why Paul didn't wave. When I see him again, I'll ask him,' she won't have any strong reaction. She may be curious, but that's about all."

Notice how many different responses were evoked from this one situation. These reactions ranged in degree from mild curiosity to severe distress. Each reaction was based on a different inference.

Now, let's consider the role of the self-fulfilling prophecy. What you predict may actually happen, not because you were right in your prediction but because inferences have great power to affect your feelings and future behavior.

If Mary makes a negative inference, for example, she is likely to feel depressed or angry. The next time she encounters Paul, she will behave in a hostile or withdrawn manner. Paul's counter response is also likely to be negative. Thus Mary's inference, "Paul doesn't like me", may ultimately prove true.

The negative inference, "It's hopeless", provides another powerful example of a potential self-fulfilling prophecy. On the feeling level, "It's hopeless", produces depression. Behaviorally, a Sit-Down Strike occurs. Without the belief that your efforts will ultimately lead to a meaningful outcome, you lose the motivation to make those efforts. The inference, "I'll never lose weight," will create enough negative feelings to retard your ability to reduce your snacks and increase your exercise.

During my work with people in therapy, I have found that the inference "It's hopeless" is *the* major roadblock to change. Until this particular message stops blaring away, a person will not take hold of the opportunities that are there and will continue to squash the budding impulses of the Intrinsic Self. "It's hopeless" puts you into the position of victim. This inference turns off the internal motor. No wonder the car refuses to run.

Positive Inferences

Making an Arbitrary Positive Inference is generally not as problematic as making a negative one. Positive inferences, in fact, can lead to happy consequences. Faith and trust, attitudes generated by positive inferences, help to buffer against the negative events in life, lowering stress and thus being beneficial to physical and emotional well-being.

When are positive inferences destructive? Like their negative counterparts, positive assumptions cause difficulty when they lead to the distortion of reality. Looking back in history, Albert Speer, in his book *Inside the Third Reich,* described how in the face of repeated defeats, Hitler continued to believe in victory: "I can only explain Hitler's rigid attitude on the grounds that he made himself believe in his ultimate victory. His religion was based on the 'lucky break', which must necessarily come his way…. The more events drove him into a corner, the more obstinately he opposed to them his certainty about the intentions of Fate."

Dr. Harvey Powelson, former director of the psychiatric clinic at the Berkeley Student Health Service, introduced me to a concept that he called "inverse paranoia." Typically, this Arbitrary Positive Inference occurs in an abusive relationship when a partner's behavior signals, "I want out" or "I don't care for you", or "I'm using you", even when verbally conveying the message, "I love you." "Inverse paranoia" involves a crucial lack of suspiciousness that keeps one hanging on. Here, the positive inference "He really loves me" or "She will change" prevents letting go. This inference is based on overweighing what the partner says, while under-weighting what the partner actually does. Again, reality is distorted.

The Antidote to Arbitrary Inferences of either sort is critical thinking. You must first ask the question, "Is this a fact or an inference?" The next step is to ask, "What are the facts supporting this inference?" Unless these facts are overwhelming, it is extremely wise to take the third step: **examine your conclusions**. This reality check can prevent your beliefs from falling off the map of actuality.

This was the step taken by Susan after she noticed that the woman directly in front of her at choral rehearsal had moved during the break to another place. As Susan tells it: "I felt my stomach turn, as I thought to myself, 'Oh, no. I must be singing off-key'. Then I remembered to check out my inference at the next break. It was hard, because I was feeling really awful, but I asked the woman why she had moved. Her reply surprised me. She explained that the man sitting next to her was singing so loudly that she couldn't tell if *she* was singing off-key. If I hadn't asked, I would have concluded that I was at fault, and I would have felt bad. Who knows? I might even have stopped attending the chorus."

Misattribution

The second Confuser, *Misattribution*, directs blame away from the real causative agent onto something or someone else. *Misattribution* is particularly toxic when applied to feelings. Many people genuinely believe that others have control of their feelings: "You made me angry" or "Talking to my friend depressed me." At some level, this feels valid. Certain negative systems or toxic people do induce feeling responses. However, to misattribute all control of your feelings to another person is to give all power to that person. If you are not a child or a prisoner, you can always leave a bad situation. It is only when you are hindered by internal obstacles that this escape becomes impossible. Natan Sharansky in his memoir, *Fear No Evil*, described how he retained the freedom of his own mind. He resolved that whatever anyone else did to him, he would only feel diminished if he himself betrayed his own values. He retained what Krishna Murti called the first and last freedom. The importance of such correct attributions is that you take back the power to control your own life. You assume the adult responsibility of taking care of yourself.

You can also misattribute responsibility for your own behavior. Abusive behavior (child abuse, spousal abuse, and self-abuse) is often blamed on something external: "I was drinking" or "I was upset by the noise" or "I couldn't take *it* anymore." In external abuse, the injured party may even be blamed for the assault: "You made me hit you. I didn't want to do it." As an abuser, you persuade yourself that you had no other choice.

The structure of language directs you toward *Misattribution*. Take the small word "it" in the preceding example. The use of this common and seemingly harmless pronoun can dismantle your own power and control.

Consider Nancy, who is thinking of completing her Master's degree. "*It* just seems too hard," she tells me. "How do you make it too hard?", I ask her. The difficulty is rarely in the task itself, but in one's driven, punishing approach to the task. Another example: Jennifer tells me about a curious feeling of panic. "*It* came over me as I was driving here today." She describes this panic right after telling me that she is debating whether to accept a new position, which has increased responsibility.

"You describe your panic as if it simply flew in the window and lit on your head. Aren't you telling yourself something with your panic?", I queried Jennifer. As she evaluated the situation more carefully, Jennifer decided not to take on the additional burden of the new demands. She recognized in her panic the Intrinsic Self warning, "No! Too much!" *It* (the panic attack) had not occurred randomly.

Perhaps the most common and painful Misattribution is the assumption that another person's behavior is the result of your own deficits. Thus, Jamie explains George's inability to make a commitment as "I'm just not pretty enough," or "smart enough," or "sexy enough," ad infinitum. Her misattribution prevents Jamie from confronting George and, if need be, from moving on. She can take self-improvement classes, try plastic surgery, or formulate any number of calculations to become "good enough". The fact remains that the desire to make a commitment and the ability to keep it rests solely with George. Men, who are dating very beautiful, smart women, still have difficulty making commitments. Just look at the cover of any recent supermarket tabloid. No amount of being "good enough" can guarantee that someone else will become a different person. This is analogous to thinking, "If *I* diet enough, *you* will lose weight."

Cognitive Deficiency

The third Confuser, *Cognitive Deficiency*, is the failure to be aware of the full picture. Many very intelligent people get caught in this Confuser, because they do not take a sufficient number of factors into consideration when drawing conclusions. *Cognitive Deficiency* creates a kind of tunnel vision. Depending upon whether you tend to externalize or internalize, this tunnel vision leads you to blame either yourself or other people unjustly.

Take Harry, for example. Harry's application for the university of his choice was turned down, leaving him ashamed and confused. Harry interprets his rejection as a notification from authority that he is not okay, that he is not competent and up to the university's standards. He makes this interpretation in spite of the fact that he has always been successful in his studies and has a top standing in his high school class.

In his thoughts, Harry focuses all of the blame for his not getting accepted on himself. No consideration is given to the large number of students applying for the few available spaces at this prestigious university or to the fact that most of the students are, like Harry, honor students at the top of their classes. He neglects to consider as well the personal and political bias that can influence any selection process. He has one factor in his equation. Acceptance equals a competent student. Rejection equals incompetence.

Were Harry to take the full picture into consideration, his equation would include all of the information listed above, and more. Acceptance would perhaps be viewed as a sum total of student competence + staff bias + number of students applying, divided by the number of spaces available + geographical location + minority status. This equation would give a more realistic picture. It would also serve as a buffer against Harry's self-punishment, allowing him to make further efforts.

If Harry tended to externalize instead of internalize, he would probably not put himself (his grades, test scores, essays, extracurricular activities) in the picture at all. He would instead focus on the flaws of someone else. "It's all Dr. Henderson's fault. He didn't take the time to write me a good letter of recommendation. That's why I didn't get in" or "That University only admits rich kids." Here the equation is also inaccurate, generating unnecessary anger that undermines future action.

Denial is a particularly pernicious form of *Cognitive Deficiency*. With *Denial*, there is not only a failure to note relevant information, but also the desire *not* to see. Openness to the full picture would lead to pain or to an undesired change in behavior. Many people deny problems in relationships, for example, because to face them would necessitate some action. *Denial* is a common companion to addiction. "I can go to Las Vegas," a compulsive gambler asserts. "I'll be in control around my business associates." Not! He comes back $40,000 poorer. It is no accident that the first of the 12 steps in Alcoholics Anonymous is the admission of powerlessness. Until the compulsive gambler breaks through his denial, he will not stop lying to himself nor will he manage his environment to prevent such catastrophic losses in the future.

The antidote to *Cognitive Deficiency* is what semanticist Alfred Korzybski called the "etcetera." The "etcetera" reminds you to account for as much relevant information as possible before making a judgment. The attitude of "What, more?" opens a narrowed focus so that you can see beyond your own belief system. I often reinforce the notion of the "etcetera" by having someone list all the possible reasons for a particular result, putting in as much information as possible into the equation. If someone's tunnel focus is generating self-blame, I ask for all the possible factors operating within another person or within the situation. If someone is directing all blame outward, I ask her to consider the effects of her own behavior. "Get the facts, ma'am," as many of them as possible.

Overgeneralization

Overgeneralization is the tendency to recognize only the similarities between people or between events and to ignore the differences. Statements like "All men are alike" or "I can't do anything right" are *Overgeneralizations*. One traumatic experience can forge conclusions about the entire world.

Overgeneralization reduces one's flexibility, one's ability to see differences, and again, one's capacity to respond to the reality of a situation. Many anger-generating messages come from the tendency to overgeneralize about another person. Statements like "He *never* thinks about me" or "She *always* complains about *everything*" generate feelings of anger and hopelessness. Notice the push toward Overgeneralization in words like *always, never, everything,* and *every time.* These words promote the distortion of reality. When such words are focused on the negative behavior of another person, they produce anger. When they relate to your own actions, they generate depression. How could a person not react to self-messages like *"Everything* I do is wrong" or "I'll *never* find anyone to love" or "I'll *always* be neurotic."

Korzybski used the methods of "dating" and "indexing" a situation as a means of interfering with the tendency to overgeneralize. Dating, which is the attaching of a time (day, hour, year) to a situation, helps you recognize that what you feel, think, and believe at one time differs from what you experience at another. The dating statement "Right now, I feel very angry with you" contrasts with the general statement "I hate you." The dated self-judgment "I wasn't a good mother to my child that month in 1994 when I was so depressed" contrasts significantly with "I wasn't a good mother."

"Indexing" means acknowledging the uniqueness of each person and each event. In other words, rather than the notion "Men are more qualified than women for upper management," the statement becomes "Man 1 (Tom) is more qualified than Woman 1 (Theresa) for Position 1 (marketing manager)." Or, "Man 1 (Tom) is less qualified than Woman 2 (Denise) for Position 1 (marketing manager)." By recognizing the differences between people and between situations, indexing allows for a more accurate assessment of reality, thereby putting us in a better position to deal with our world.

Vague Language and Either/Or Thinking

In his book *People in Quandaries,* Wendell Johnson describes two additional Confusers, *Vague Language* and *Either/Or Thinking,* which lead to great unhappiness. He notes how frequently the "good things of life" are described in vague words like *success, happiness, wealth,* and *accomplishment.* Of course, these terms encompass many specific events that differ for different people. Success to one person may mean making over $50,000 a year. For another, success may mean becoming a millionaire before the age of thirty. Of course, the first person is likely to attain the good feelings that come from a self-acknowledged success, more than the second, whose criterion is so much higher.

Because it is such a vague concept, many people do not have a clear-cut definition of happiness, experiencing it as an elusive, never-to-be-captured experience. Although Sara has many positives in her life (money, property, advanced degrees, friends, recognition), she does not consider herself happy. When the Confuser, *Either/Or Thinking,* is added to *Vague Language,* Sara's thought chain expands from "I'm not happy" to " I must be a loser." The final result is a great deal of self-evaluative pain.

When a marriage ends, there is a strong tendency to engage in *Either/Or Thinking,* adding self-generated distress to what is already a painful situation. The partners in a divorce may consider that they are failures. Yet often both partners have experienced significant growth during the marriage. Author and therapist Shirley Luthman once said that people frequently use a marriage to grow up. When this growing up process is completed, there may be a need for the partners to go their separate ways. Certainly such a marriage was not a "failure" in the total sense in which that word is so frequently used.

Actually, there is a great amount of territory between success and failure. In acknowledging that there is a huge middle ground, one needs to learn to be specific and to think in percentages. Thus if you make the statement "I haven't accomplished anything this year," you probably mean, "I haven't accomplished 100 percent of what I think I should have accomplished." If "what I should have accomplished" is defined clearly, and you want to break out of the *Either/Or Thinking* structure, then you can report, "No, I can't really say I've accomplished zero percent. It's more like 50 percent or 60 percent." This new perspective attacks the view "It's either 100 percent or nothing," where everything from 1 to 99 percent doesn't count. Thus, Carl reports, "I didn't finish editing my book last year. That was my goal. But I did complete seven of the chapters, and I can feel good about that."

Magnification and Discounting

The seventh and eighth Confusers, *Magnification* and *Discounting*, describe how we either overestimate, or underestimate, the importance of a person or a situation. These Confusers allows you to retain your basic beliefs at the expense of reality. Thus, if you have a negative self-view, you will survey your every move with a microscope. If you see your self-worth in terms of physical beauty, you will give far too much emphasis to a blemish or an extra pound. If you are basically unsure of yourself, you will magnify the importance of a failed sexual encounter. Similarly, any positive compliments or achievements will be viewed through the opposite lens and quickly discounted or forgotten. As I frequently tell my clients, you have no "Velcro" for anything positive, but I see you picking up a lot of negative lint.

Magnification can cause tremendous stress. When you place a life-or-death importance upon a decision (whether to take one job over another, whether to live alone or with a roommate, or whether taking a leave of absence is the "right" thing to do), you generate so much anxiety that action of any kind is blocked. A misunderstanding or a disagreement with your mate can be magnified into the end of the relationship. If you operate by *Magnification*, you live on a stormy sea, struggling to overcome each approaching wave.

The antidote to *Magnification* is the active process of "bringing it down to size." "It" refers here to the situation, be it the importance of a decision, the catastrophic consequence of an action, or the difficulty of a project. "Bringing it down to size" may involve discussing the particular problem with someone who is not involved. It may mean waiting until the next day to take action. It frequently involves breaking a huge project, which rests ominously on the horizon, into small workable steps. Time itself is a wonderful antidote to *Magnification*. Give yourself a "night to sleep on" any decision. This allows natural clarification and sorting, and the problem either disappears or assumes a more realistic weighting.

Discounting, on the other hand, requires a different antidote. Knowing that within a short time you will forget your positive actions or the accolades you have received, place these **on the record**. Secondly, ferret out any discounting self-talk. A statement like, "Oh, she's my therapist. She has to say something nice," or "I'm sure he tells that to everyone." discounts both you and the other individual. Yes, there are con artists, but there are also people who can genuinely affirm the positive in you. Allow this corrective emotional experience, especially if you were raised by a narcissistic parent or had overly critical mentors.

I/You Messages

This chapter would not be complete without discussing one additional approach to combating Confusers. This approach involves the use of *"I"* Messages, a technique first emphasized by Dr. Thomas Gordon in his book *Parent Effectiveness Training. "I"* Messages state feelings and opinions. They differ from *"You"* Messages, which primarily use negative labels to attack and undermine.

In communicating assertively with other people, *"I"* Messages are much more likely to be received positively than *"You"* Messages. Think of how differently you react to "You're wrong" versus "I disagree". Or, consider the *"You"* Message, "You're insensitive," compared to the *"I"* Message, "I feel upset when you're late for our tennis date".

The shift from *"You"* Messages to *"I"* Messages is more than a practical communication tool to be used when interacting with other people. It is a vital focus for creating a new form of self-communication. When incorporated at a deep level, *"I"* Messages will give you the vehicle to alter your view of yourself.

Take Betty, for example. Because she is lonely and bored, Betty goes out with a guy she really doesn't like and returns from her date even lonelier than before and angry with herself to boot. Her usual *"You"* Messages to herself are "You are so stupid.", "You just can't learn.", and "You were an idiot to go out with him". These messages need to be replaced by *"I"* Messages to herself. She might conclude, "I don't want to go out again with someone I don't like just because I'm lonely and bored. I need to make my life more interesting so that I'm less vulnerable to acting against my real wishes." Notice that these *"I"* Messages do not get Betty off the hook with herself. They simply stay with the facts and with Betty's feelings, as close to the behavioral level as possible. Negative judgments are avoided. Why? It is simply because they do not help, and because they actually make most situations worse.

Within these negative judgments, "You are so stupid", "You just can't learn", and "You were an idiot to go out with him" are traces of all eight Confusers.

Betty's statement to herself, "You just can't learn.", is an Arbitrary Inference. How many times has Betty been out with this guy anyway? One time? Does this really constitute "not learning"?

What does Betty mean by *stupid* anyway? Her *Vague Language* is a rather severe self-punishment for the specific crime of going out on a date and failing to have fun.

Do you see Betty's *Either/Or Thinking*? She is telling herself that either everything works for her, or she's stupid. There is also *Magnification*. Betty's one date, which lasted all of five hours, is construed as so important that it constitutes the universe's final opinion of her intelligence and character. Finally, we see *Cognitive Deficiency*. Betty's tunnel vision is causing her to overemphasize the negative. What about all the decisions she has made that were positive? Don't they belong in the equation as well?

Most of us, like Betty, live in that neighborhood somewhere down the hill from perfection. Some of us are pleased when we progress forward. On the other hand, many of us are angry because we are not already on top. Do you see any progress as a reminder of your own deficiencies rather than as a signal of your own accomplishments? The old adage of the glass of water sitting on the table applies here. The optimist describes the glass of water as half full; the pessimist sees it as half empty.

By now, you can see just how closely related Drivers, Stoppers, and Confusers are in their negative effects upon the Intrinsic Self. I separated them initially to give you a clearer understanding of each process. In reality, the self-dialogue combines bits and pieces of each to build a strong case against simply being you. Based on the particular set of *shoulds* and *should-nots*, which form your pattern of basic beliefs, the Drivers, Stoppers, and Confusers of the Imposed Self band together to reinforce a particular theme.

If you have grown up believing that the opinions of other people are very important, that not making waves is preferable to standing up for your own self, and that self-worth comes from other people's approval, you will be propelled by the Driver, *Please Others*. Any tough parts of the Real Self, such as anger, independent strivings, or intellectual rigor, will be stopped with Negative Labels like "impolite", pushy", or "rude". Catastrophes about rejection and disapproval will surface.

Along these same lines, if you have the Driver, *Be Strong*, you will experience self-hate and humiliation when any soft feelings are exposed. Softness will be labeled as "weakness", and sadness called "self-pity." Caught in the *Be Strong* constellation, you will magnify the amount of time spent in sharing sensitive feelings. To illustrate, one man who had shed all of five or six tears during one therapy hour concluded that he had better pull himself together before he completely collapsed.

Now that you can recognize your own Drivers, Stoppers, and Confusers, it is time to begin the second section of this book. Here, you will learn a step-by-step procedure for changing your internal dialogue. If you choose, you can move from a repressive and dictatorial inner companion to one who allows for self-nourishment and personal growth

CHAPTER 5

Changing Your Tapes

Help!" I'm drowning in a sea of judgments," Sally shared only half-jokingly. "I can see Drivers and Confusers all around. I'm smothering with Stoppers. What do I do now?"

Maybe you're asking yourself a similar question. Short of exhausting yourself with marathons, distracting yourself with a movie, or involving yourself in a new love affair, how do you deal with the self-talk shark swimming through your life?

There is an answer. There is a simple, direct, and effective five step method of ejecting your negative Judge and substituting a supportive new coach and internal guide.

The Five-Step Method

Step 1: Be Aware. Listen to your own self-talk.

Step 2: Evaluate. Decide if your inner dialogue is supportive or destructive.

Step 3: Identify. Determine what Driver, Stopper, or Confuser is maintaining your inner speech.

Step 4: Support Yourself. Replace your negative self-talk with Permission and Self-Affirmation.

Step 5: Develop your Guide. Decide what action you need to take, consonant with your new supportive position.

The following five questions will allow you to put this method into practice:

1. What am I telling myself?
2. Is my self-talk helping?
3. What Driver, Stopper, or Confuser is operating?
4. What Permission and Self-Affirmation will I give myself?

5. What action will I take based on my new supportive position?

Steps one, two, and three help you to separate yourself from your Imposed Self and create distance from the edicts of your Judge. You must get out from under that dark cloud hanging over your head with its thundering warnings and lightning accusations. The questions: "What am I telling myself? "Is my self-talk helping?" and "What Driver, Stopper, or Confuser is operating?" will allow you to gain this distance. Let's examine these first three questions in detail.

Step 1: Be Aware.
What Am I Telling Myself?

Listen carefully to your own self-talk. This is the first step toward changing it. Most likely, you are not aware of the automatic tapes that control your life. Like the self-instructions that gradually fade into the background when you learn to drive a car or use a new computer program, your self-talk goes underground. You are left with unexplained feelings but no awareness of the internal decisions causing them.

Fortunately there are areas where your self-talk is most likely to be accessible. These involve external triggers, such as compliments, criticism, new projects or activities, and periods of intimate sharing. Internal triggers also open the door to your inner landscape. Feelings, physical symptoms, and avoidance tendencies are all harbingers of negative self-talk. You can use both external and inner events to discover something about your own inner speech.

Compliments

How do you respond to a compliment? When someone tells you, "You look nice today" do you respond, "Thank you, I feel good today," or do you discount, "Oh, my hair is getting too long. I've got to get it cut". If your work is praised, do you apologize, "If I had had more time, I would have polished it a bit more," or do you affirm, "I'm really glad you like what I did. I've been feeling good about this project myself." The way you respond to compliments gives you a beginning awareness of your inner speech.

Criticism

How about external criticism? For many, the pain of criticism comes not so much from the attack by another person but from your own internal response to the attack. For example, when Claire's husband asserted, "I don't think the house is clean enough to have people over after the meeting tonight?", Claire shouted back, "I know this house isn't clean. I'm just not a good housekeeper. I'm messy. Okay, I know I'm messy. There's nothing I can do about it." In other words, Claire magnified tenfold any critical message directed toward her. I asked Claire, "If someone throws a stick at you, should you pick the stick up and beat yourself with it?". She laughed, "No. I guess not.". How do you handle the stick?

New Projects and Activities

Drivers, Stoppers, and Confusers are summoned by new projects with ferocious intensity. When I ask members of a class to write down situations where their self-talk is negative, someone usually confesses, "I know of a situation where I treat myself badly, but I notice that I'm punishing myself even as I'm writing it down. I'm thinking, 'Will this be boring to the class? Is my situation too personal? Is this what you want?' My Judge is everywhere!" Begin looking at your internal response to new situations. You too may find your negative self-talk more pervasive than you ever imagined.

Intimate Sharing

Sharing your intimate feelings with another person or with yourself in a journal is a fourth way to discover negative self-messages. When I ask a client, "What did you say to yourself when such and such happened?" I will often hear something like, "I told myself that I was a coward" or "I decided that I acted really stupid". Some confess, " I babbled like an idiot when I talked to my date" or "I found out that I'm inept at playing handball." These self-deprecating comments cause bad feelings. Yet until they are brought out through conversation, they go unrecognized.

Feelings

Your feelings actually provide the best single path to your inner speech. By feelings, I am referring to bodily sensations of anger, joy, sadness, remorse, excitement, or lethargy. I am not referring to disguised self-judgments such as, "I feel that I am stupid" or "I feel that I can't do anything right." Negative feelings are frequently signals of negative self-talk. A sudden shift in emotion, particularly one that seems to occur out of the blue, signals that you have just said something to yourself.

This happened to Cheryl one evening when she returned from a conference where she had been one of the featured speakers. Just as she was about to put her key in the door, she felt what had been a sense of elation suddenly disappear. "It was almost like a trap door opened, and I fell from my pleased, positive mood to feeling really down," Cheryl related. "This happened all in what seemed to have been a two-second period. I wasn't dreading going home, as far as I knew, so I asked myself, 'What is going on here? What am I saying to myself?' The answer was right there, once I asked the question. I had been feeling good about my speech, thinking to myself, 'That was the best speech I've ever made. Everyone seemed to like it.' Then I asked the question, 'Will I be able to keep this up?' That was when my depression began."

Unexplained feelings of anxiety, lethargy, or hostility, as well as sudden bursts of energy and enthusiasm, almost always rest on a hidden internal statement. Ask yourself the crucial questions: "What am I telling myself?"; "How am I scaring myself?"; or "How am I depressing myself?" If you ask and take the time to listen to your replies, the messages of your Imposed Self will surface. Once they do, start writing them down. Keep a record of your own self-talk. This will give you examples to work with as you make your shift to self-support.

Physical Symptoms

Symptoms such as a stomachache, difficulty in breathing, a rapid heartbeat, or sweaty palms are additional clues to negative self-talk. Over the years, the correlation between mind and body has popped up in phrases like, "You're a pain in the neck" or "This job is a real headache." For Robert, feelings of anger are bypassed and translated directly into physical pain. This pain is Robert's signal to ask the question, "What am I telling myself?" In answer to his question, Robert finds that he is tolerating a situation that is toxic to him. His roommate has reneged on his part of the rent this month. By disguising with pain his own legitimate anger, Robert has had no action signal to motivate an assertive response.

Muscular tension is another signal of negative self-talk. Such tension often manifests a conflict between a feeling and the self-talk that prevents that feeling from emerging. In his book *The Disowned Self,* Nathaniel Branden says, "A child discovers very early, often wordlessly and subconsciously, that he can deflect his awareness away from the undesired feelings, and further, that by tensing his body and constricting his breathing, he can partially numb himself to his own state."

Thus, many people smile as they describe painful or humiliating experiences from their pasts. The smile serves the delusion that it is really not so bad, even as it prevents full awareness. As people become conscious of this process and the accompanying self-talk that upholds it ("You're not so bad off; other people have worse experiences; don't be a big baby," and such), they are able to let go and to experience for the first time feelings of rage and sadness that have been blocked. These feelings, along with the childhood messages in which they are wrapped, then become available for examination.

Ira Kamin described this kind of experience in his article "Dropping the Smile for Awhile:"

"When I first started going to therapy, I was in such pain I was numb. I told my therapist horror stories. I told him I felt like someone was twisting my arm behind my back. I told him I was getting pinched twenty-four hours a day. I told him I couldn't stand the pain, even though I couldn't feel it anymore.

He said, 'Do you realize you've told me all this with a big smile on your face?'

'No,' I said....

It took me less than a summer to cry with my therapist."

Permission to drop the smile is unfortunately not always available. At the first sign of distress, many people respond with the pseudo-supportive statement "Don't cry" or "Don't feel bad" or the punishing prohibition "Stop wallowing in self-pity." If you do not contradict such messages, you will squelch your feelings and lock a huge part of yourself away inside the tension of a smile.

One evening, while I was feeding my cat and the raccoons, which visited each night, I noticed myself having difficulty breathing. I immediately asked myself the question "What are you telling yourself?" I quickly realized that I was pushing myself to hurry up and get everyone taken care of. I was walking rapidly and rushing up and down the stairs with a tense preoccupation with getting everything done. Naturally, my breathing reflected the fact that my Drivers were going full blast. When I gave myself permission to take my time, my breathing returned to normal. I was able to stop only when I considered my physical symptom (difficulty breathing) to be a possible signal for negative self-talk.

Many people do not permit this possibility and instead attribute any physical reaction to something entirely different. An anxiety-based stomachache is interpreted as cancer, generating still more tension. Psychogenic chest pain is considered the beginnings of a heart attack. Even when medical tests show that no physical problem is present, a person may deny that negative emotions can provoke physical pain. When the stress-related symptoms actually lead to physical damage, a psychosomatic condition such as an ulcer results. The underlying unrecognized factor is all too often negative self-talk.

Avoidance Thoughts

When you find yourself thinking, "I have to get out of here," "I want to go back to bed," or "I need a drink," ask yourself if you are attempting to escape from the internal pressure of negative self-talk. Thus, Sally found herself fantasizing about going away to a desert island. "Maybe then," she told herself, "I could get some letters written and some books read." Sally was trying so hard to please others that she had no time for herself. She suddenly realized why her Intrinsic Self wanted to transfer to a desert island.

The same dynamic was behind Jim's "I wish I were dead" rumination. "I'm really not suicidal," Jim explained. "I just keep having the thought, 'I wish I were dead.'" As Jim became aware of how he was pressuring himself with the underlying messages, "You've got to succeed" and "You've got to make it this year", the grip of fear loosened. The next time Jim had that thought he was able to tell himself, 'I'm more important than making it this year." He turned his suicidal thought into a warning signal that he was exerting too much self-pressure.

Avoidance Behaviors

Have you ever found yourself eating, having a cigarette, or curiously eager to clean the house rather than confront what you have actually chosen to do? Glenda was clearly procrastinating when she outlined, "I spend hours cleaning out a drawer or straightening up my desk. It seems I'll do anything to distract myself from what I really want and need to do, which is to call about a job." Glenda's delaying behaviors keep her from confronting her underlying negative self-talk. Messages like "They won't be interested." "I'm not sufficiently prepared." or "I'll sound incompetent" are generating the anxiety that leads to her avoidance.

The following exercise will help you to discover your negative self-talk. It will also disclose your best signals for uncovering your inner speech.

1. Think of a recent compliment. What was your reply?
2. What criticism have you faced lately? Did you add to it and make it worse?
3. List a new project or activity. What did you tell yourself as you started or failed to start it?
4. What beliefs about yourself have you shared in intimate conversation? Were these beliefs negative or positive?
5. Think of a situation (time, place, surroundings) where you felt negative about yourself. What did you say to yourself while in this situation?

6. Do you have any common physical symptoms? What are your symptoms telling you?

7. Do you find yourself engaging in "wishful thinking?" Do you often procrastinate? If so, from what negative self-talk are you escaping?

This exercise is not an easy one. Each question takes significant time and thought. If you draw a blank in responding, you may wish to follow the suggestion I gave to Debbie who couldn't make sense of her behavior.

After losing six pounds, Debbie began breaking her diet plan and eating more than usual. She felt terrible about herself, but had no idea why she had gone off her diet. She concluded that she was masochistic and really didn't want to lose weight.

After assuring myself that Debbie's increased consumption wasn't based on a reaction to a starvation regime (a common occurrence that plunges many dieters into a diet-binge pattern), I asked her to shut her eyes and replay the day she had begun eating more than she had planned.

"I was feeling really well," Debbie began. "I had lost six pounds and had bought a new dress that I actually looked good in. I was excited and wanted to see exactly how much weight I had lost that day. When I got on the scale, I saw a two-pound *gain*! At that point, I told myself that I was just fooling myself, that I was never going to lose weight, and that it was unfair that I had been so good and had gained two pounds. I was furious. I felt like throwing the scale across the room. Instead I started eating."

By replaying the events of her day, Debbie discovered that she had been totally unaware of her negative self-talk. This discovery allowed her to understand those other occasions when she had reversed her weight loss after reading her scale. Now she has a clear enemy in the line of fire for the next step.

Step 2: Evaluate.
Is It Helping?

If you answer "No. What I'm telling myself isn't helping at all", you begin to disengage from your negative inner speech. Once you recognize that you are generating feelings of anger, depression, and anxiety, while undermining your problem-solving ability, you can challenge your Judge with a sense of personal authority and conviction.

Do not ask yourself, "Is my self-talk true?" or even "Is my self-talk realistic?" You will believe these pronouncements and so remain stuck in the judgmental framework. Carl's Judge warned him that he hadn't accomplished anything for the past ten years. "That's true," Carl exclaimed and settled even more firmly into depression. "Maybe so," I replied, "and if you keep listening to your Judge, ten years from now you can tell yourself the same thing. Your Judge has prevented you from using your talents and abilities by just this kind of self-talk. The question is not 'Is it true?' but 'Is it helping?'"

As you begin to realize that your own self-talk leads to negative consequences, specify exactly what these consequences are. Try the following exercise. From your previous list of self-messages, choose several typical examples. Then ask yourself, "Is what I am telling myself helping?" If your answer is no, see if you can determine what the negative costs are in each of the five basic areas: feelings, behavior, self-esteem, interpersonal relationships, and level of stress. If you like, compare your responses to those in the two situations that follow.

Situation 1: Squelching Yourself.

Charles has been invited to a friend's party and, although he hasn't any other plans, he is hesitant about going. He has an all-too-familiar litany of excuses. He decides to consider their effects.

"What am I telling myself?"

"I'm telling myself that there's no reason for me to go to Jan's party. I won't meet anyone there, and I'm just no good at small talk. I'll be boring, and it will be boring.

Is this self-talk helpful?

No!

How is it affecting my feelings?

That's clear. I'm getting really depressed. I feel lousy.

What is the effect on my behavior?

I won't go to the party, so I'll just sit here alone all night.

How does my self-talk relate to my opinion of myself?

I'm putting myself down with what I say.

How is my self-talk affecting my relationships with other people?

To be sure, it's not helping me meet anyone new. My friends are going to get tired of my never showing up at their parties.

What about my level of stress?

I feel conflict when I'm so pessimistic, because I would like to go to the party and have a good time. I guess I'm making my stress level go up."

At this point, Charles can evaluate the various costs of his negative self-talk in very clear terms. Understanding these costs will help tilt his decision in the direction of his own growth.

Situation 2: Pressuring Yourself.

Penny's best friend Sharon has experienced a severe depression. Penny invited Sharon to spend several months with her. Penny now finds that she herself is quite distressed. She examines her self-talk.

"What am I telling myself?":

"I am asking myself, 'Should I have taken this on?' I'm not always able to talk with Sharon. What if I make things worse? I should do more for her. I don't have enough time. How can I tell the difference between helping and interfering?'"

Is this self-talk helping?

No.

What is the feeling cost?

I'm feeling confused and afraid. I'm going to get depressed myself if I don't stop beating myself up about this.

What effects does my self-talk have on my behavior?

I overextend myself and later resent it. I don't set limits. Then I withdraw.

How does it affect my self-esteem?

Instead of feeling positive about helping Sharon, I feel bad about myself. I can never do enough.

What about my relationships with others?

Being over-solicitous and then withdrawing is confusing to Sharon. I'm not helping her by feeling so guilty.

What is my stress cost?

It's really high. Again, I can see that I'm going to be depressed myself if I don't let up."

Try the exercise with one of your own examples. Your self-talk may affect you in only one or two of these five areas. However, the clearer you are about the cost, the more motivation you will have to change your negative messages. There are three additional examples at the end of this chapter that illustrate the complete answering of the question "Is my self-talk helping?"

Step 3: Identify.
What Driver, Stopper, or Confuser is maintaining your inner speech?

When you determine the specific Driver, Stopper, or Confuser on which your self-talk is based, you uncover the underlying beliefs, which fuel your negative inner speech. You simultaneously direct yourself toward a positive alternative.

You create a springboard for change. Thus one person decides, "Here I am telling myself that I have to *Try Hard* to send everyone I know a Christmas card. I don't have to do that. It's okay for me to let go of that demand this year. It simply doesn't fit with the fact that I'm now working." Another realizes, "I've been calling myself *lazy* all day. I have the right to do nothing sometimes. This is my day off. I'm not going to spend it *Hurrying Up*."

When Jessica realizes, "There I go again, trying to be the Bionic Woman," she gains further distance from her *Be Strong* Driver. When Gary decides, "I rarely assert myself when I feel stepped on, because I tell myself that I'm being *picky*. That's a negative label. I don't have to let it control me anymore," a large part of that his assertive problem has been eliminated.

The shift in your self-talk will inevitably affect what you do, feel, and believe. When you move from negative to supportive self-talk, your feelings will lighten; you will become more assertive, less driven. As you alter your self-talk, you actually set up a corrective mechanism for challenging the entire structure by which you live your life. As changes in self-talk lead to changes in behavior, the external environment responds to support your growth. The following situations, one involving a Driver, one a Stopper, and one a Confuser, illustrate how this works.

Situation 1: Diffusing a Driver.

Gayle has been on a diet for several months. Although she has lost quite a bit of weight, she hasn't yet met her goal of 135 pounds. Lately her diet hasn't gone very well. She has, in fact, exceeded her calorie limit on a couple of occasions. Gayle suspects that the culprit is the fear that she will not meet her weight loss goal by the time she and her husband take the Hawaiian vacation they have planned. Gayle wants to turn off this mounting pressure.

Question: "What am I telling myself?"

Reply: "I'm saying, 'If you don't start losing weight faster, you won't be thin enough for your trip to Hawaii. You promised yourself that you would look good."

Question: "Is my self-talk helping?"

Reply: "No. This pressure is making me feel anxious, which means I eat more. I'm seeing myself as a failure. I'm getting irritable with the kids. Pressuring myself is making me gain weight, not lose it."

Question: " What Driver is operating?"

Reply: "It's a clear *Hurry Up*. There's also some *Be Perfect* in there. I can't go to Hawaii unless I look perfect."

Question: "What Permission and Self-Affirmation will I give myself?"

Reply: "I will allow myself to take my time. Even if I go to Hawaii at this weight, I'm fine. After all, I've lost enough already so that I look okay in shorts. If I get off my back, I'll start losing weight again."

Question: "What action will I take in response to my new Permission?"

Reply: I'll take a walk tonight. Also, I'll tighten up on the food I buy so I'm not tempted to blow my diet. And I will do something nice for myself besides eating. This self-punishment has been depressing."

Situation 2: Squelching a Stopper.

Jeannie is beginning to feel that her life is passing her by. Except for work, she rarely goes out. Although she has ideas of what she might like to do, somehow she never manages to carry them out. One idea is to transfer to another location. Jeannie has not acted on this impulse, however. She decides to find out why by exploring her own self-talk.

Question: "What am I telling myself?"

Reply: "I'm saying to myself, 'I'd like to transfer to my firms San Francisco office.' Then I think 'Oh, come on, Jeannie, you're doing it again. It's just another pipe dream. You're being silly. San Francisco looks good from a distance, but once you get there, you'll be unhappy again. Everyone's going to think, 'There she goes again, living in a fantasy world.'"

Question: "Is my self-talk helping?"

Reply: "No. It's keeping me isolated and depressed. It's stopping me from trying out new things."

Question: "What Driver, Stopper, or Confuser is operating?"

Reply: "I'm stopping myself by calling my idea a *pipe dream,* by labeling myself as *silly,* and by saying that if it doesn't work out I'll be *wrong.* I'm also catastrophizing that other people will disapprove and that they won't like me."

Question: " What Permission and Self-Affirmation will I give myself?"

"I will tell myself that it's okay to have fantasies and dreams. I will also say that if I find out that San Francisco is not what I want, I'm not wrong. I've simply learned something new on which to base my actions. I'm a levelheaded person as well as someone who likes to dream. It's okay to let my friends know the dreamer part of me."

Question: "What specific action will I take to help me resolve my problem?"

"I'm going to make an appointment to talk with Human Resources about a transfer. Then I'll decide my next step."

Situation 3: Confronting a Confuser.

Craig has been laid off by his start up company. He just learned this week that his application for a particularly desirable position in another firm has been turned down. Craig responds with anxiety and depression. He finds himself procrastinating about applying for other jobs. He begins to explore his own self-talk.

Question: "What am I telling myself?"

Reply: "I'm saying that I will never find another job in my field."

Question: "Is my self-talk helping?"

Reply: "No. I'm getting so fearful of rejection that I don't even feel like looking for another job. All I'm doing in my spare time is sitting around feeling bad."

Question: " Is there a Driver, Stopper, or Confuser in operation?"

Reply: "I'm drawing a negative conclusion about what's going to happen. Telling myself 'I'll never find another job' is a Confuser. I've made a negative inference. The fact is that I didn't get the job I wanted. That doesn't mean that I won't find another."

Question: "What Permission and Self-Affirmation will I give myself?"

Reply: "I'm a qualified person. I do good work. I have special skills that a lot of companies can use. It's okay for me to assume that I will get a job, at least until I've given it a better try."

Question: "What action do I want to take to help me achieve my goal?"

Reply: "I've got a stack of resumes sitting on my desk ready to be sent. If I stop assuming it's hopeless, I'll feel more like mailing them. I'll make myself the goal of sending out at least one a day. That doesn't seem like much but sending seven out this week is a lot better than the zero I sent out last week."

CHAPTER 6

Learning the Language of Self Support

Supportive self-talk is like French or Italian or Japanese, a new language to master. Fluency takes a little time and practice. These final two steps will take you to a different country within yourself. This new relationship begins with Step Four: Supporting Yourself through Permission and Self-Affirmation.

Step 4: Supporting Yourself.
What Permission and Self Affirmation will I give myself?

Let's listen to Elizabeth's struggle as she attempts to replace her judgmental self-talk with a new language, one oriented toward growth.

ELIZABETH: "I recently ran for city council and lost by some three thousand votes. I keep torturing myself with the idea that maybe I could have won, if I had received the endorsement of a particular community organization. At least, I should have tried to get it."

PAMELA: "Elizabeth, would you describe out loud what you usually tell yourself about losing the election. Only this time, also go through the five steps involved in changing your inner tape."

ELIZABETH: "My negative talk usually starts out, 'Elizabeth, you should have asked for the support of the Commission. If you had made any effort, the other candidate wouldn't have received their approval. You were really dumb not to go after it. The Commission only endorsed so-and-so because he asked, and you didn't.'"

PAMELA: "That's enough of the negative. It's clear that you're aware of punishing yourself. Move on to Step 2."

ELIZABETH: "Let's see. I'm to say to myself, 'I need to step back a moment. Is what I'm saying to myself helpful?' No. I am depressing myself by dwelling on something that's over. I can't do anything about it now. As to

Step 3, I suppose I'm trying to *Be Perfect* again. *(Here Elizabeth's tone and pace suddenly changed. She rapidly continued.)* Anyway, there's a real question as to whether or not I did do the right thing. Actually, the Commission should have invited me to speak to them, so that they could hear both candidates' views. They shouldn't have been so biased. He probably promised them something for their endorsement."

GROUP: *Laughter*

ELIZABETH: "Besides, I did give three speeches each week, and I knocked on three thousand doors."

PAMELA: "Would anyone like to give Elizabeth feedback? Was what you heard self-support?"

The group's consensus was that Elizabeth had effectively gone through the first three change steps (being aware, determining the destructiveness of her inner speech, and recognizing the Driver in operation). However, she had not developed and expressed any genuine support for herself. Instead, Elizabeth was *blaming* and *justifying*. She blamed the Commission for not inviting her to speak and justified that she hadn't had the time to appeal to them anyway.

By what she said, Elizabeth demonstrated that she had not, in fact, escaped from her judgmental position. In shifting blame from herself ("You should have asked for their support") to the community organization ("They should have invited me to speak"), Elizabeth remained in the right/wrong framework. The only difference now was that the organization, not she, was at fault. Of course, Elizabeth's feelings also changed with the shift in the focus of her blame. She was no longer depressed; she felt angry. The group's laughter occurred exactly at this point of emotional transition. Unfortunately, while anger may feel better than depression, shifting blame will not allow Elizabeth to let go of this old situation or of her negative feelings.

Elizabeth's comment, "Besides, I did give three speeches each week, and I knocked on three thousand doors", is an example of justification, a second way the judgmental position masquerades as self-support. Distinguishing justification from self-support is difficult. There is, however, a difference, a very important one. Justification explains away negative self-talk while at the same time upholding the judgmental belief upon which it is based. Self-support, on the other hand, demolishes both the self-talk and the underlying belief.

When Elizabeth made the comment "Besides, I did give three speeches each week," her voice signaled that she was not supporting herself. Even the introductory word "besides" indicated that an excuse was in the offering. Elizabeth clarified her message when she observed, "When I made that statement, I was still trying to convince myself that I *was* perfect by justifying what I had done. I just don't want to give that up, do I?"

Based on the feedback she had received and her own increased awareness, Elizabeth began again. This time, in a firm solid voice, she stated, "I deserve credit for running in the election, whether or not I did everything perfectly. I got nine thousand votes; and I established an effective election committee. It's okay for me to be proud of myself."

Elizabeth's last statement *was* an example of self-support. By stepping outside the Imposed Self's standard of perfection, she affirmed herself and acknowledged her own growth. This time, the listing of her accomplishments held no hidden motives. Her self-support included both Permission and Self-Affirmation.

Permission

Webster's dictionary defines Permission as "giving an opportunity." Giving yourself Permission gives you the freedom to make mistakes, to have feelings, and to experience yourself as human, all without self-punishment. Paradoxically, by giving yourself this flexibility, you insure that you will function at your highest level of effectiveness.

Subjectively, Permission is experienced as a relief, as the lightening of a burden. This relief can be very important for someone struggling under the depressing weight of negative self-talk. Richard, for example, had the cleanest office anyone could desire, but he had not written a page on his novel for over three months. The thought of sitting down at his desk was enough to knot his stomach and convince him that he needed a drink.

After taking him through a standard relaxation procedure, I asked Richard to imagine himself beginning to write, making sure to remind himself that he was just jotting down ideas and that he need not try to make his writing sound perfect. Moreover, I suggested that he was in no hurry at all. He would have plenty of time to rewrite and revise later. All he wanted was to put his ideas down on paper. After he had written for ten minutes or so, he was to allow himself to do something pleasant like sit in a hot tub, have a cup of tea, or read a magazine.

Richard was able to visualize this scene with no increase in tension. Afterwards he offered, "In the way you described it, beginning to write was like entering a soft space. I could go on like that forever." Replacing his Drivers with Permissions created the soft space, which Richard spoke of. "It's okay to take your time" and "It's okay to make mistakes" substituted for *Hurry Up* and *Be Perfect*.

I've often thought of self-support in terms similar to Richard's soft space. To me, it brings to mind the idea of a pillow cushioning a fall, or a protective buffer that absorbs and dilutes any external assault. A similar analogy appeared in an article about addiction written by psychologist Nicholas Cummings. Cummings likened a person addicted to drugs or alcohol to "an unfinished house that has only an attic and a basement." In confronting an obstacle, the addict falls "from the attic straight to the basement," running "quickly to the bottle, the pill, the needle. So, indeed, the first thing we have to teach is how to build a floor in the house, because you cannot live just in elation or depression." In our terminology, this floor is built with Permission and Self-Affirmation.

Let's review for a moment the basic Permissions that oppose Drivers, Stoppers, and Confusers. Briefly, these Permissions are:

It's okay to be human; it's okay to make mistakes.
It's okay to follow my own pace and to take my time.
It's okay to listen to, honor, and act upon my own feelings.
It's okay to please myself.
It's okay to support myself and to allow myself to succeed.
It's okay to say *no*.

All Permission has at its core the decision to honor and trust the Intrinsic Self. Such trust may go against what you have been taught, bringing up fears of being "selfish" or not a "good person." Moreover, it goes against the common notion that other people's feelings are more important than your own.

When I made a similar statement to Sharon, one of my clients, she responded strongly, "But I can't follow my feelings. They have always gotten me into trouble."

"Are you sure about that?" I asked, "Aren't most of the decisions you regret based on going against your feelings?"

After some thought, Sharon agreed. "Yes. I married a man I didn't want to marry and stayed in that marriage for five years because I was afraid of my feelings. A month before the wedding I knew that I wanted out, but I didn't want to disappoint my mother. "

Even when you start to operate from this new supportive position, one foot may remain behind, stuck in the old judgmental mold. Listen to Mitch, during a group exercise, when he began to make the leap toward self-support.

"I want to take up scuba diving," Mitch asserted. "I've wanted to do it for a long time, but I tell myself that I shouldn't. It costs too much; it's dangerous; it's not productive. I don't know anyone else who's into diving, so

I would be doing it just for me. I'm too old to start something new like that. Everyone will think I'm crazy."

Mitch's assignment was to counter his negative self-message and to substitute a positive, supportive one. He began Step Four: "I guess I could say to myself, 'Taking up scuba diving may not seem productive, but actually a lot of ideas can come to a person when he's away from his desk and just relaxing. Even though it would be just for me, I might not be so depressed all the time, so I would be better company for my family. Maybe I'm not too old. It might be good for me to get the exercise.'"

During the group feedback, several class members praised Mitch. "You were able to turn around the objections you listed and see a positive side to each of them," one person said. "That sounded better." another offered. But even as Mitch was being given positive feedback, Allison seemed disturbed. "It sounded to me like your scuba diving has got to be productive in order to be okay," she countered. "In other words, unless scuba diving is going to let you solve some work problem or improve some relationship within your family, you can't justify doing it. Sounds to me like you're still into *Please Others* and *Be Perfect*. What about scuba diving just for fun?"

In one sense, Mitch had fallen into the same trap with his scuba diving that Elizabeth had been caught in earlier with regard to her political defeat. He was trying to appease his Imposed Self with the assurance that his diving would not be contrary to its internal commands. Mitch had not really asserted the Permission, "It's okay to please myself."

Once his self-talk was truly based on this Permission, Mitch stated, "It's important for me to listen to my insides and to nurture myself. I have the idea that I would enjoy scuba diving, and that's reason enough to try it. It's okay to do it for the sheer pleasure that it could bring. Whether I become more productive, or a better husband and father, isn't relevant. It's okay to do it for myself."

There are three additional Permissions that deserve special consideration because of their special difficulties. These are: (1) the Permission to Need, (2) the Permission to Accept Limitations, and (3) the Permission to Feel Good.

The Permission to Need

Although sex is out of the closet, having needs is not. A strong taboo exists against needing other people. The very idea provokes intense reactions: "Can't you use another term? Neediness sounds so desperate."

The message, "Do your own thing", produces the general assumption that if you need another person, you simply do not have your act together. Yet, there is no life without need. An inanimate object differs from an animate one based on need. Plants need sunshine. People need other people. As Simon and Garfunkel immortalized in the hit song, *Sounds of Silence:* "Rocks feel no pain, and an island never cries." If you need desperately, it is usually an indication that you are not allowing yourself to act in ways that meet your needs. You are stopping yourself with your own self-talk, with some rule or label, and making yourself into a victim.

In one group, I asked the members when they first learned to feel shame about having needs. Jane replied with strong emphasis, "The starving Armenians. As a child, anytime I felt sorry for myself or needed anything, I was reminded of how ungrateful I was. At least I had food on the table, had two legs, and two eyes. Ungrateful. That is the main block that I have to being needy."

Stan admitted, "I simply learned not to ask. I kept my needs to myself. My attention was always on making my mother happy. I grew up with a dominant mother, and then I married a dominant wife. I have no concept of needing anything, except perhaps relief."

Elisa added, "If I want and get something, other people will be jealous. They won't like me. In my family, there was never enough to go around. There was not enough affection or attention or love. If I got something, my sister went ballistic."

The idea that neediness is shameful prevents positive moves toward its resolution. Taking a class, joining a support group, or buying a pet, can fill all or part of the void created by loneliness. Then, you can approach seeking an intimate relationship from fullness, not starvation. Without shame, you can answer a personal ad or join a dating service, a modern necessity for some in a world of cubicles and anonymity.

A very dear friend once told me a story about a red hat. I have repeated the story many times to clients, who are struggling with the issue of neediness. Here is the story.

"Once upon a time a woman decided that she wanted a red hat. So she went to a store and asked the salesperson to show her a red hat. The salesperson replied, 'I'm sorry, but we don't sell red hats at this store.' Now, instead of immediately leaving the store and going to another one, the woman began a rather common internal dialogue. 'I bet if I just wait awhile, they'll get in some red hats.' So she waited and waited until the store was about to close. She even decided to come back the next day, and the next. Over time, as she thought further, she figured that maybe she was not quite attractive enough for the salesperson to sell her a red hat. She began a self-improvement course, lost some weight, and cut her hair. Still, no one in the store produced a red hat. She became very sad at this point and began to cry. Looking desperate, she secretly thought to herself that if she were sad enough, someone just might round up a red hat. She saw other people go past the store wearing red hats, but this just convinced her that she must try all the harder to make herself 'good enough' to deserve one. Somehow, she never thought to believe the clearly stated assertion, 'We don't sell red hats!'"

This story had a profound effect on me at the time. I was dating a man who had said to me, even before we got involved, that whenever a woman fell in love with him, he always fell out of love with her. He was, in other words, not available for a love relationship. He didn't sell red hats.

I have told the story with several variations. One variation is that the woman doesn't even tell the store clerk what she's looking for. She doesn't ask whether the store sells red hats. It hardly matters if someone has told her up front, "I don't ever want to be married," or "I don't love you." Her illusory self-talk keeps her hanging on to a depriving situation with the hope, "If I'm good enough, you'll change." The inner child from the past is hoping to win the unavailable parent's love by trying hard, so very hard, one more time. It is a certain setup for a relationship *not* to work.

Permission to Accept Limitations

A famous commercial tells us, "Just do it!" Teachers and pundits throw out, "You can have it all." These injunctions put limitations in a shameful light. Because *everything is possible*, any shortcoming is a negation of your very self. Yet limitations are a fact of life.

As John Bradshaw writes in *Healing the Shame that Binds You*, "We humans are essentially limited.... Healthy shame is the basic metaphysical boundary for human beings. It is the emotional energy, which signals us that we are not God—we need help too. *Healthy shame gives us Permission to be human.*" (Italics mine)

Illness offers us permission to have and to assert limitations. One aspect of physical illness, in fact, is an automatic "time out" from the demands of the Judge. In their study of cancer, the Simonton group, authors of *Getting Well Again,* asked their patients to list any positive aspects of having cancer. The patients freely acknowledged five benefits: (1) Having permission to get out of dealing with troublesome situations or problems; (2) receiving attention, care, and nurturing from others; (3) having the opportunity to regroup psychologically to deal with a problem or find a new perspective; (4) finding incentives for personal growth or for modifying undesirable habits; (5) not having to meet the high expectations of themselves or others. Notice how much these benefits have to do with permission to have needs and to accept limitations.

The Permission to Feel Good

In writing my first book, *Self-Assertion for Women,* I remember working on a particularly witty section and experiencing a growing sense of elation and excitement, upon which I immediately got up and went downstairs to make myself a cup of tea. It was almost as if I could not allow myself to feel that good.

Many people lack this important and basic permission to feel good. Do you manifest the cultural superstitions that tell you the "Evil Eye" will punish any signs of happiness or wellbeing? Do you avoid sharing your success with your friends, fearing you will hurt or antagonize them? Do you refuse to enjoy what you have, believing that it will instantly vanish, if you acknowledge your assets and accomplishments?

George feared, quite simply, the experience of loss. If he never allowed himself to have anything, so his thinking went, he would be spared the pain of losing it. This thinking is, of course, a lie. George will still have to face all of the grief that life brings. He will simply have forfeited the joy.

I continually see people entering self-talk loops which take them away from the happiness of the now—fear loops, depression loops, regret loops. "I treated my daughter so badly when she was little" begins the regret loop. Three hours later, Sara is still running around in that loop, generating anxiety and depression, and helping no one because she cannot change the past. How much more desirable is a current train of thought like, "How can I amend my behavior toward my daughter now?".

Many philosophers have emphasized the value of honoring the moment, seeing this as one of the essential keys to happiness. I recall one of my happiest times, when I was on my horse. He was eating grass, while my head was lying across his neck. I was looking at the tiny wildflowers around his nose. The sun was shining. My Judge was asleep. I was free, simply to be.

Self-Affirmation

Self-Affirmation is a positive declaration about your own self. Its focus is on growth. Because Self-Affirmation is tied to the Intrinsic Self, it may make little sense when viewed in terms of other people's values. Thus, to the amazement of her friends, a woman with the Drivers, *Hurry Up* and *Try Hard,* may affirm herself for choosing to take more time off, rather than for accepting a prestigious or financially rewarding assignment. A man with a *Be Strong* Driver may regard his newfound ability to cry as a major growth step, one opposing the stifling message of his past, "Take it like a man."

Self-Affirmation requires you to look within to your own center to decide when and how to support yourself, reflecting the adage: "It's not where you are on the track that counts. It's where you started and how far you've come.".

Jamie related two instances in which she had attempted to affirm herself. In the first, she experienced her negative feelings evaporate as she completed the final steps of the tape changing method. With her second attempt, she did not fare so well. She could not neutralize the depression she experienced over her inability to assert herself with two people at work. In fact, as she found the tape changing method not working, Jamie felt even more depressed.

Because she had written down her answers to each question in the five-step method, I was able to examine her responses very carefully. Nothing caught my attention until I came to Step Four. Here, Jamie gave herself Permission to take the long time it seemed that she needed to become more assertive. She told herself that is was okay to be slow about it, and she affirmed that she would try to give herself credit for even tiny assertive steps.

Her judgmental perspective revealed itself in the terms *long time, slow,* and *tiny.* As we talked, Jamie was able to say, "I'm patronizing myself, patting myself on the head. I'm saying, 'It's okay for you to be backward.' I guess I'm so used to judging myself that it creeps in even when I'm trying to be supportive."

Jamie was still judging herself. She had a preconceived notion of how much time she should take to master the task of being assertive. Jamie only focused on how much she was lacking. As with most judgmental standards, Jamie's were not actually realistic. She was setting as arbitrary time limit on very difficult changes. Moreover, her judgmental view kept her from recognizing how far she had come. She did not appreciate the fact that by asserting herself she had already solved a number of problems in her love relationship.

As Jamie came to realize, it would have been surprising if she had found herself feeling better after completing the five-step process. Her Permission and Self-Affirmation were tainted with subtle judgments. As such, they could not neutralize the effects of her original negative statements.

While it is important to affirm yourself for *doing,* as Jamie attempted in giving herself credit for her newfound assertiveness, it is also imperative to acknowledge the okay-ness in just *being.* What psychologists have termed *unconditional positive regard* relates to this basic affirmation of the Intrinsic Self. Simply stated, this means that whatever you choose to do for others or not do for them, whatever perfection or lack of it you manifest in your work, whoever loves you or doesn't love you, you are worthwhile. Your self-worth is not based on externals, but on the unique individual you are, an individual who may not have been nurtured or appreciated in the past, but who was and remains okay. While people can and do engage in destructive behavior towards themselves and others, this is usually based on underlying shame and rage, defended against by shamelessness and an inability to admit mistakes.

By talking directly to the little child who is still within, you permit the emergence of feelings of love and compassion and the decision to support and protect that precious part of yourself. When Amy spoke to the little five-year-old girl inside, her whole manner changed: "You're a beautiful, lovable child, whether or not you please your mother. You don't need to keep trying so hard to get people to like you. I'm not going to allow you to tolerate a bad environment." Amy's expression to herself here is true Self-Affirmation.

As you now begin to support yourself through a new and possibly foreign language, the following guidelines will prove useful:

Forget What Should Be: Give yourself credit for the steps you have taken, without judging their size or weight. Don't require a major breakthrough for self-acknowledgment. Change often follows an exponential curve. The first small steps can be ten times more difficult than later larger ones.

Be Specific: When you spend two hours on a project, give yourself credit for two hours. Don't say, "I spent some time on writing."

Focus On Something Besides Accomplishment: Stated more positively, praise yourself for effort, for improvement, for allowing yourself to express or to experience your feelings. Give yourself credit for being aware of a negative process, even if you have not yet changed it.

Learn To Think In Percentages: If you reduce your negative self-talk by 10 percent, then you have made a step forward, even if you are still overly critical 90 percent of the time.

Encourage Yourself: Remind yourself that you are a valuable and lovable person right now, whether or not you accomplish, improve, or change anything.

The following comparisons illustrate how Self-Affirmation works within a growth framework. Note that Self-Affirmation finds no place within the Judgmental Position.

Situation 1: Dealing with Conflict.

Susan and her husband, Jim, have spent the last week fighting about Susan's desire to accept a promotion in her firm. The new position will require Susan to travel several days a month, and Jim doesn't want her to be away from home that often. Describing her week, Susan says:

JUDGMENTAL EVALUATION: "Jim and I aren't compatible. None of my friends has a husband as rigid and traditional as Jim. But I guess my friends aren't as cowardly and wishy-washy as I am either. We just don't have a good marriage."

GROWTH EVALUATION: "It has been a difficult week, but I think that Jim and I have become clearer about each other's feelings. Not long ago, I would have given in at the slightest indication that Jim didn't like something. This time I've stuck to my position, in addition to hearing his."

Situation 2: Taking New Risks.

Joe has taken on a project that requires knowledge of several new accounts. In order to complete this assignment, he finds that he must ask other people in the office for specific information. This is new for Joe, who has always prided himself on his independence. Describing his problem, Joe says:

JUDGMENTAL EVALUATION: "You're in over your head here. You should have mastered this by now. I bet the guy before you wasn't such a dunce. Your coworkers probably think you're a poor manager."

GROWTH EVALUATION: "It's hard for me to ask questions, but I think it's positive that I'm doing so anyway. I don't think I could have asked for help a few years ago. I would have made mistakes and suffered through a lot of unnecessary trial and error. I'm finally turning off that *Be Strong* Driver."

Situation 3: Being a Beginner.

Eleanor is taking a class in public speaking to help her master her fear of giving oral reports at work. Having just completed her first speech, she says:

JUDGMENTAL EVALUATION: "That was bad. You stumbled three times; you dropped your notes; you didn't gesture once. Everyone else gave a much better speech. Your topic was too technical. They didn't understand half of it."

GROWTH EVALUATION: "Hey! One down and ten to go, you did it, kid. That was hard for you, but you did it. The important thing was not how it sounded (you can improve on that later). The important thing was that you got up there and made a speech."

Notice that each judgmental evaluation began with the premise of perfection and then demonstrated what was wrong with each person's effort. There is little chance for good feelings to derive from this stance. Like the little girl one teacher told me about, who was upset about her test score of 98, you may obsess about the two points missed rather than acknowledge the 98 points received. The growth model, on the other hand, is capable of generating tremendous positive feelings. Since there is no arbitrary expectation, any progress, any step forward, is acknowledged and appreciated.

The judgmental position may be the only one you have ever known. Your self-talk quite naturally flows from it. This is the freeway, the default mode. To oppose this habitual flow is monumental. Barbara Gordon's book *I'm Dancing As Fast As I Can* gives an example that reflects some sense of the magnitude of this struggle. After spending her birthday away from the hospital where she was working to overcome her psychological and Valium-induced problems, Gordon returns, "filled with a heady sense of accomplishment." She elaborates: "That night before I fell asleep, I said to myself, 'You did it, Barbara.' But my exhilaration was interrupted by a crack from my smart-ass self, that mocking, negative part of me that wouldn't let me alone. 'Terrific,' she said. 'Next week you can go to sleep-away camp.' I tried to silence her and remember the day. The struggle between the two of me must stop, or I won't be able to live."

This struggle between the Intrinsic Self and the Imposed Self, between the judgmental and growth positions, will invariably begin when you make the transition from your old language to the new. What was once underground will surface with a frightening intensity. As Gordon describes it, "I was forty-one, engaged in a battle with myself tougher than any fight I had ever had. Melodramatic or not, I would have to fight as hard for me, and against me, as I did against the bad guys. If only I knew how to do it."

Pick a situation and try out for yourself the judgmental and the growth evaluations. Determine which feels better, which motivates you for the future.

For those of you having difficulty with the growth evaluation, you might try talking to yourself as you would talk to another person. Dr. Geraldine Alpert, a close friend and colleague, shared with me the question she asks her clients who are not supporting themselves: "What would you say to a child whom you loved if he or she were to have made the kind of mistake you just made?" An entirely new set of responses is called into play when a problem is broached from the perspective of talking to a loved one. Dr. Alpert then goes on to ask a second question, "How about being as good a parent to yourself as you are to that child?"

Creating a Buffer

Self-support creates a protective barrier against the inevitable toxic situations or destructive people in your life. Nowhere does Epictetus's maxim, "Man is troubled not by things, but by the view he takes of them" apply more than here.

By definition, a buffer is a shock absorber, a protection against outside influences. The buffer provided by your own self-support will stabilize you and keep you centered in the face of disappointment, criticism, rejection, or disapproval. Equally important, a buffer of self-support can protect you from the critical Judge of someone else.

Everyone has received destructive feedback from another person at some time in his or her life. If you lack a protective buffer, you risk going under in the face of negative feedback. Author Ayn Rand received fifty rejection notices before *The Fountainhead* was accepted for publication. It subsequently sold millions of copies. Would you have persevered under similar circumstances? With a buffer of self-support, you could have. Rejection never feels good, but with a buffer or cushion, it simply doesn't have to feel so bad.

The first time I was aware of creating an internal buffer for myself, I was teaching a class on child development. I presented a fairly technical lecture on learning theory and its application to behavioral problems in children. At the break, several students approached me and criticized my topic as being "too technical" for them. I was able to listen to their criticisms and make some changes, making the class more rewarding for them and easier for me. What pleased me most, however, was that my own self-talk cushioned me from any destructive internalization of their criticism. For a *Be Perfect, Please Others* individual like myself, this was no small feat.

The buffer I used was the internal reminder "I'm okay even if I'm not liked and approved of every minute. I don't have to be a perfect teacher." I repeated this Permission to myself even as these students were sharing their concerns. I won't go so far as to say that I enjoyed the criticism. I can say that I didn't get particularly depressed or upset about it.

It is important here to emphasize that a buffer does not block incoming information. (I heard the students' criticisms and made some of the changes they requested.) Neither does it throw the criticism back and counterattack. (I did not turn their objections around and accuse them of being lazy or unwilling to work.) A buffer simply neutralizes the judgmental component inherent in most criticism. It allows the information to be received and dealt with while minimizing any self-evaluative pain. Instead of picking up the stick that someone has thrown and beating yourself with it, you learn to pick it up, examine it, use it constructively, or throw it away.

When therapy is successful, a person comes to a point that often seems incomprehensible when viewed from an outside perspective. The environmental stress that originally brought the person into therapy may have remained unchanged. The process of altering the stressful situation may even have stirred up more immediate difficulty (a quietly toxic marriage may be moving through a turbulent divorce). Yet the inner environment is vastly altered. When in the face of equal or additional stress, you feel congruent, alive, and calm within yourself, you know that a genuine turnabout has occurred. A cushion has been created. A buffer has been constructed. Self-support has become a basic ingredient in your internal psychological structure. You are speaking and living a new language.

CHAPTER 7

Developing Your Guide

Once the *Be Perfect* dieter affirms, "It's no tragedy when I don't stick to my diet one hundred percent. It's okay for me to be human. I've already lost five pounds, and I'm doing well.", she has changed her critical, punishing orientation to a supportive one. If she is not careful, however, her Judge will again dominate "Well, don't get too confident. One mistake is all you get!" Reverting to the old standard is a dangerous possibility.

On the other hand, it is not in the dieter's self-interest to eat a fourth handful of potato chips or move on to a bowl of ice cream. A direction is necessary, a *plan* for action. You know the negative consequences of the *Be Perfect* tightrope. What you need is a sidewalk, a flexible path that allows for mistakes yet moves in the desired direction. To help you to make this transition, you will need a Guide.

Step 5: Develop Your Guide.
What Action Will I Now Take?

In contrast to the Judge, a Guide helps you to formulate an action strategy that is both realistic and useful. Developing this Guide is the fifth and final step involved in changing your tapes. Let's compare the Judge with this new Guide, starting first with the attributes of the Judge:

The Judge ignores your Intrinsic Self. It operates totally on preconceived notions of what *should be*.

The Judge is inflexible. No change is allowed because of altering circumstances or feelings.

The Judge does not consider the environment. Again, it operates within the rarefied atmosphere of "what should be" and ignores "what is."

The Judge knows nothing of small steps. The message "Do something" is never amplified by the instruction "This is the first step." There is no help in breaking a task into bite-sized pieces.

The Judge relies on Drivers, based on the assumption that you would not move if you were not pushed.

The Judge uses punishment, not reward. Its focus is on what is lacking, not on what is accomplished.

Let's now examine the Inner Guide:

Your Guide takes into account your Intrinsic Self: your feelings, your day-to-day fluctuations in mood, your changing priorities and desires.

Your Guide is flexible. It allows your action plan to vary with changing circumstances.

Your Guide considers the environment in which your particular behavior is to be developed. This environment is then altered as part of the action plan, if necessary.

Your Guide is satisfied with small steps. Rather than demanding you to accomplish such and such, your Guide asks, "What step can you take to move forward in your growth?"

Your Guide does not permit Drivers to interfere with your action plan. There is no *Hurry Up*, *Try Hard*, or *Be Perfect*. Your Guide assumes that given the proper environment, you will grow in the manner that is best for you.

Your Guide incorporates ample positive rewards into each step along the way.

Referring back to the initial example, the dieter's Guide might say, "It's likely that you ate those potato chips because you let yourself get too hungry and had nothing else on hand to eat. The next time you're going to be at school late like this, bring a balanced snack with you. Then you'll have something good to tide you over, and you won't be so tempted to hit the vending machines."

Notice that when the Guide is functioning, a workable plan is set forth, a sidewalk approach to meeting the stated goal. The dieter's hunger is not criticized or ignored. It is taken as an important need that must be integrated into any workable plan. Also, notice that special measures (bringing a balanced snack) are considered necessary because of the special circumstances (being at school late in the evening) that the dieter faces. Working with the realities encountered rather than ignoring them is an important function of the Guide. Instead of, "Just Do It," the Guide formulates, "This is how you *can* do it."

Your Guide gives you the vital tools of: (1) taking small steps, (2) being sensitive to the environment, (3) having sensitivity to your own feelings, (4) providing ample self-reward, and (5) being self-assertive. Because skill in applying these principles is very important, we will now consider each of them in detail.

Small Steps

One of the simplest principles your Guide employs is the use of small steps. Dorothy Tennov, the author of *Super Self,* suggests that a step "should be large enough to be discernible, small enough to be accomplished." If a step is too large, it will be avoided. If it is too small, it will go unnoticed.

Most of us err by making our steps too large. In writing a report, we decide to complete it in one six hour block. We diet by setting a five-pound weight loss goal each week. We list twenty items to accomplish in one day. Of course, the larger the step, the less likely we are to meet it, and the more we set ourselves up for discouragement and self-punishment.

After having a very difficult time finding an exercise that she *would* do, Jane decided to apply the Small Step principle. It originally seemed to her that she was using this principle when she told herself that it was okay to jog only once around the track. She thought she was using it when she gave herself permission to go to just one aerobics class each week. But these behaviors dwindled away to nothing. Jane finally recognized that as small as these steps might seem to her Judge or to another person (a quarter-mile jog is certainly a minute step to a twenty-six-mile marathoner), they were too large for her.

Therefore, Jane decided to find an exercise that was indeed a small step, one that would start her moving toward her goal of becoming more physically fit. Living in a house with three flights of stairs, she decided that running up and down two of the flights might be a good place to start. She tried this out and found that running three times in a row, up and down the stairs, felt okay. Over the course of two weeks, her batting average hovered around .500. "That's okay," she told herself, remembering that *Be Perfect* usually ends in *Do Nothing.*

The practice of making one's first step small enough seems simple. Yet, it frequently goes against the Judge's *Hurry Up, Try Hard* command. When anxiety is great, a first step may need to be small indeed. One of my clients, for example, set as her first step the goal of simply counting the pages of the chapter she was supposed to read. Once she looked at it, her fear lessened enough for her to move to the second step of reading the chapter headings.

Many problems, which loom huge and frightening on the horizon, become manageable when the steps are made small enough. If you are avoiding some task or ignoring a goal, your problem may simply be that your first step is too large. Break it down. Continue cutting the demand until your first step becomes one that you can make without depression or dread. Once you have finished this step, you can renegotiate with yourself about the next one. Along these lines, consider how you might apply the small step principle to housecleaning, writing a paper, beginning an exercise program, or making a career change.

If your first step in housecleaning is something on the order of "clean the bedroom," you have probably *not* made your step small enough. Cleaning the bedroom is in itself composed of many steps: vacuuming, making the bed, picking up clothes, and dusting. If you happen not to be in an energetic mood, your "clean the bedroom" command will leave you sitting on the couch watching one more television program. A better step might be "Hang up five items in the bedroom."

When it comes to writing a term paper, the Judge will tend to demand, "Stop bellyaching, sit down and write it." A Guide, on the other hand, might offer, "Read and underline the first article on the topic. Don't try to decide what you're going to write yet. Just read the article." If all of the material has been read, a Guide might suggest, "Jot down five questions that you want to answer in your paper." Or it might ask, "What's the easiest section to write? List your ideas about that section." Notice that these steps gently lead the reluctant writer into the material. Usually, this brief exposure will prove sufficient to capture the writer's interest. Sometimes more will actually be accomplished than the small step would indicate, but that is not the goal. If a "fire" does ignite, that is just icing on the cake. If it doesn't, the writer will still be one step ahead.

Sensitivity to the Environment

When Jane chose to exercise by running up and down the stairs, she made certain that this exercise could be accomplished in her own home. Although she lived near a track, experience had taught her that the effort involved in driving there and back was simply too great to maintain her exercise program, which was still very low in habit strength. Again, she decided that it was better to do something at home than do nothing on the track. This choice involved sensitivity to her environment.

If you are to be maximally effective, you must develop this sensitivity. Unfortunately, if you have a strong sense of how something ought to be, you may fight your environment rather than use it for your own benefit. You may expect yourself to have "self-control" under any circumstances and punish yourself if this control disappears in the face of strong environmental demands.

In working with people who want to lose weight, I often find this strong need to deny the reality of environmental influence. People expect their weight to fall off with ice cream in the freezer and cookies in the cookie jar. They expect themselves to push aside the hot bread and butter sitting on the table in front of them. They want to continue cooking for the family in all the regular ways. Yet weight loss comes from controlling in advance any tempting foods, not by having them available.

Sensitivity to the environment is important with most other goals too. If you want to improve your grades or become more productive in your work, you must keep any non-work distractions to a minimum. For Nola, sensitivity to the environment required constructing a workspace for herself. The hassle of getting out her sewing materials, making a space for herself on the dining room table, then having to clean up in preparation for dinner meant that Nola avoided sewing, which she really enjoyed doing once she got down to it. The purchase of an inexpensive secondhand table and the assertion of her need for a permanent area made it possible for her to pursue her goal. Once she had squelched her Judge's "you should be able to work anywhere" belief, constructing a supportive environment was simple.

Sensitivity to Your Feelings

The third hallmark of an effective Guide is sensitivity to the feelings and needs of your Intrinsic Self. This includes two different aspects: sensitivity to your moment-to-moment feelings and sensitivity to your current capability level. Sensitivity to your feelings involves the willingness to listen carefully to your own inner experience. Many people have learned not to trust their insides. They ask others, "What should I do? What decision should I make?" rather than listening to their own feelings. Yet relieved of the muddying effects of Drivers, Stoppers, and Confusers, your feelings give you the clearest, most complete feedback possible about your own unique direction.

When I was a child, my grandmother and I used to play a game where one of us would search for an object that the other had chosen somewhere in the room. When the object was being approached, we would give the progressive feedback "You're warm; you're getting warmer; you're hot; you're hotter; and you're almost on fire!" The opposite message was broadcast when the object was being evaded. The immediate feedback that was so much a part of this game is analogous to the role your feelings have in guiding your direction.

When you allow yourself to operate in conjunction with your Intrinsic Self, you will invariably experience a sense of unblocked flow. You will often feel excited, happy, energetic, or enthusiastic. You may also feel angry or sad or tired, and if you do, these feelings will be accepted and supported. You will allow yourself to experience them fully and finish them, so that you will not accumulate resentment in your gunnysack or block your expression of grief through depression and muscular rigidity. In short, you will not experience the conflict that occurs when you are fighting with yourself.

When operating through your Intrinsic Self, you will listen to and honor your feeling signals, whatever they may be. If you are relaxing in the sunshine, you will not need to tell yourself to get up. You will act when your feelings signal your readiness to do so. Since you are not on a Sit-Down Strike, your basic energy pulse is alive to activate you whenever a thought or an external issue captures your interest. Similarly, because your experience of grief or anger is neither fueled nor squelched by the messages of your Imposed Self, your emotional expression becomes a healing and time-limited experience. As one person having connected to the power of her feelings for the first time exclaimed, "I just can't stop talking about all my plans and new ideas. I feel so excited. I never thought that I could be this happy."

Just as feelings of aliveness and oneness inform you that you are on the right track, anxiety, depression, and lethargy tell you that you have either wandered away from your own feelings, or that you are fighting against them. The now well-known experiments by Stanley Milgram on obedience to authority give us a dramatic example of this latter process. Milgram's studies examined the amount of electric shock a subject would willingly administer to another person when instructed to do so by someone in authority. In a result that baffled and outraged many people, Milgram found that a majority of subjects (62 percent) obeyed an authority's command, even to the point of delivering what was thought to be 300 volts of electricity to another person.

Of interest to us is the fact that the subjects delivered the shock over their own "powerful reactions of tension and emotional strain." As Milgram notes, "Persons were observed to sweat, tremble, stutter, bite their lips, and groan as they found themselves increasingly implicated in the experimental conflict." Very few subjects, however, listened to, or acted upon, their own internal emotional responses when authority demanded, "You have no choice; you must go on."

This same unwillingness to honor one's feelings occurs in less startling examples as well. Commonly, while dieting, people refuse to recognize that hunger must be kept at a manageable level. In fact, accepting the validity of hunger is one of the most important factors in a successful weight loss program. Paradoxically, I often ask people on diets to eat more at breakfast and at lunch so that by the end of the day their hunger will not precipitate a "to-hell-with-it" binge on any and everything available in the house. The "Zone" diet has served me well in keeping my hunger within manageable levels.

Depression is another signal that frequently indicates that we have lost touch with the needs of the Intrinsic Self. The woman I mentioned before, who was experiencing a newfound excitement about her plans and activities, had been depressed for several years. Her feelings were telling her that her needs were not being met. As her Stoppers were neutralized, she began again to engage in the outdoor activities that she had once enjoyed. Then she reevaluated her work situation, made some changes, and her depression lifted. Operating in a manner similar to physical pain, her depression was the signal that told her to change directions.

Sensitivity to Your Capability

A sensitive reading of your capability level is vital information for your Guide. If you are a person who says, "Don't ask me to do anything, until I've had my third cup of coffee," you are speaking of a low morning capability level. The comment "After six o'clock, I'm too pooped to do anything except watch the tube" demonstrates sensitivity to a reduced capability at the end of the day.

In *Super Self,* Dorothy Tennov distinguishes "five levels of capability, from most capable (Level One) to least capable (Level Five)". Level One capability involves the capacity for peak performance. This is the level at which you can do your best work, tackle your most difficult projects, do your hardest thinking. Alternatively, Level Five is good for relaxing or for doing, at most, routine tasks. Capability levels are based on recurring physiological cycles, such as sleep, or hormonal fluctuations, as well as transitory influences, such as illness, depression, fatigue, or even good news.

It goes without saying that the Judge has little sensitivity to or sympathy for our differing capability levels. The *Be Strong* battle cry is "full steam ahead," regardless of the internal feedback. *Hurry Up* ignores any need to pace your self. Alternatively, a rigid requirement like "Before you start your project, get your desk cleared off" can underutilize your high energy level. Folding clothes or answering routine letters while you're raring to go at Level One will set you up for failure. Similarly negative expectations ("It's probably a pipe dream") can take the fizzle out of your Level One enthusiasm. In short, both over-employment and underemployment of your current capability level can lead to negative outcomes. One vital function of your Guide is to match your internal level with the external demands that you face.

Many of the clients whom I see have set themselves up for self-punishment by having a lack of sensitivity to their own current capability. They attempt to do complex, high-level tasks while at low energy levels, and failing, consider themselves "incompetent", "lazy", or "stupid". Moreover, a lack of self-nurturing combined with an overabundance of Drivers frequently results in a general reduction in overall capacity. If you push yourself to extreme excess, you will become depleted, depressed, and burnt out. You will experience *Exhaust Time*.

Exhaust Time, the lowest level of capability, *can* be pleasurable, but only if self-demands are kept to a minimum. Exhaust Time is for sitting in the sun, reading for pleasure, taking a nap, or doing nothing. It is a time for restoration and self-nourishment. Many people don't believe in Exhaust Time. They operate as if it didn't exist. The same insensitivity to the environment, which we found earlier, occurs to this inner state as well. Worse still, many people punish themselves for any low-level capacity. This self-punishment can dampen a naturally lowered energy cycle and push an individual into depression.

If you expend a great deal of high-level energy on work, you may be allotting only Exhaust Time for yourself or for your mate. A working couple, who get together only during periods of Level Five capability, will not find their relationship to be fun and romantic and exciting. By the weekend, when they finally are out on the town together, is it any wonder that their conversation is dull, and that sex later on is an unimaginative, routine affair? They are both exhausted. The allocation of Exhaust Time for personal pursuits frequently leads to mediocre results.

Joe, for example, works as a tax attorney. Actually, he overworks. Sixty to seventy hour weeks are the norm for him. The time that Joe has left over after work is mainly Exhaust Time. He spends it playing racket ball, puttering around the house, and reading books about his own financial planning. Joe doesn't find much time for developing a relationship, which he says is his top priority. He generally doesn't feel like socializing on Friday or Saturday nights since he has worked all day. He never has time for lying on the beach, browsing around a museum, or going to a new place where he might meet someone.

Although Joe punishes himself for not getting out more ("What's wrong with you? Have you lost interest in women?"), he lacks the desire to do so. Joe's work takes all of his high level time, leaving him without the energy for any social stimulation. The effort involved in meeting new people is simply too great to occur at Level Four or Level Five capability.

At the end of a weekend, during which he has worked nine or ten hours, Joe criticizes himself: "Another weekend blown. You're not going to meet anyone unless you get out more. Why didn't you go to the party Friday night?" As Joe looks at his internal message, he asks himself:

Step 1: "What am I telling myself?"
Reply: "I'm telling myself to stop making excuses and get going."

Step 2: "Is my self-talk helping?"
Reply: "It might help if I said it on Friday afternoon. On Sunday night, no, it doesn't help. It depresses me."

Step 3: "What is the Driver, Stopper, or Confuser?"
Reply: "Try Hard. I tell myself that I shouldn't want to lie around here all weekend. I should be out trying hard to meet someone."

Step 4: "What's my Permission and Self-Affirmation?"
Reply: "That it's okay to listen to my own feelings and act upon them. That means I can relax and do nothing if I want. I deserve some time for me."

Step 5: "What is my Guide, my action plan?"
Reply: "I'm going to stop working for awhile on Saturday. I'm going to relax all day and see if I feel like going out on Saturday night. I'll let a few people know I'm interested in meeting someone and see what happens. Maybe it's time to talk to my boss about an assistant. One thing's for sure, unless I have more time to unwind and recuperate, I won't get out."

Notice that Joe's action plan is based on sensitivity to his capability level. This sensitivity necessitates that Joe change his environment (by increasing his time at home) to give himself an opportunity to pursue his goal of forming a relationship. The same may be true for you. Whether your goal is to take time to meet someone, to write a book, or to develop a new interest, there must be enough available energy for you to function in these areas at a high Capability Level.

Ample Reward

"Use the carrot, not the stick," the old adage goes. The use of reward rather than punishment can motivate without creating negative side effects.

You can use self-rewards to increase desired behaviors and to decrease unwanted ones. You can use them to study more, to smoke less, or to learn to dance. Rewarding yourself will produce changes that will simply not occur if you are motivating yourself with *shoulds* and self-punishment.

There are two aspects to rewarding yourself. First, in and of itself, positive reinforcement will help you to maintain a high level of psychological functioning. Just as you need food for physical energy, you need to nurture yourself for maximum psychological health. You can do this by providing a generous supply of internal and external rewards. Second, positive reinforcement allows you to reinforce yourself after the completion of each step in your action plan, insuring that your new behavior will be maintained and strengthened.

Reinforcement and General Well-Being

When I see clients who are depressed, one of the first things that I examine is the number of enjoyable activities in which they are currently engaged. Usually, there are few such pastimes. Most have been replaced by self-imposed work or family demands. There is virtually no time to listen to music, to read a novel, or to go swimming.

This was the case with Suzanne. When she was promoted to merchandising manager in her firm, Suzanne found herself with very little free time. As her unit was expanding, a heavy burden of reports fell to her, along with the continuing demands of supervision, budgeting, and planning. After several months of operating at a whirlwind pace, Suzanne began to feel depressed. When her co-workers started to notice, she decided to begin therapy.

In talking to Suzanne, it immediately became clear that she had three Drivers constantly in operation. They were *Be Perfect*, *Hurry Up*, and *Try Hard*. Her *Try Hard* Driver, in particular, led her to keep her hands in every facet of her unit's activities. Suzanne could not set priorities because to her Judge everything in her unit was top priority. She had to meet each demand (*Try Hard*), to meet it at once (*Hurry Up*), and to maintain a top level of performance (*Be Perfect*). The result was long hours under high stress.

When Suzanne came home, frequently with unfinished paperwork in her briefcase, she was too tired to go for a walk, to experiment with a new recipe, to do her needlepoint, or to write or telephone friends. Her lunches with fellow professional women, once a major source of enjoyment and support, had dwindled to once or twice each month. In fact, one by one, all of Suzanne's sources of reinforcement and self-nurturing were set aside.

Fortunately, Suzanne was able to look objectively enough at what was happening to decide to arrange her life in a different way. Once she realized how stagnant her life had become, she immediately made plans to have dinner with several friends. Purposefully, she arranged these meetings early enough to force her to leave work at a regular time. She stopped carrying any paperwork home. "I never do the work anyway," she explained, "but I tend to feel so guilty about not doing it that I don't listen to music or read a novel or do something that I might actually want to do."

As Suzanne began to treat herself better, her depression lifted. Interestingly, the fulfillment of her actual job requirements did not suffer. The ever-so-exact reports weren't missed. She still conveyed the information needed, but with much less time and energy spent on making them perfect. She learned to delegate responsibilities and found that letting go of some of her control did not lead to total collapse. Her staff's morale actually improved. In short, Suzanne developed a Guide who considered self-nurturing a very necessary ingredient in fulfilling her long-range goals.

Reinforcement and Positive Behavior

When any behavior is followed by a positive consequence, that behavior is strengthened. Rewards, even small ones, are important motivators for habit change. I can well remember how effectively my piano teacher used rewards during my first year of lessons. Upon the successful completion of a piece of music, I received an animal sticker to place in a paper circus car. For my nine-year-old self, this was a very big deal indeed.

The same motivating effect will occur when you reward yourself. When Gail followed her thirty-minute walk with lunch, she walked much more frequently than when she moved to an office with no lunch facilities nearby. When Jimmy allowed himself to have a beer with his friends after studying for two hours, he found himself ready to hit his books soon after dinner. When Betty gave herself a point every time she avoided the impulse to smoke and cashed her points in for small articles of jewelry, clothing, and cosmetics, she found that her withdrawal didn't feel so bad.

The more a habit change involves some kind of deprivation, the more vital is ample reward. In her book *I'll Never Be Fat Again,* Eda LeShan writes, "Nothing turned out to be more important while dieting than learning to comfort and reward myself with gifts other than food. Here's (my) journal entry: No weight loss for two days, and I'm feeling discouraged and sorry for myself. I stopped at the drugstore and bought myself an assortment of makeup I certainly don't need. I felt like an idiot until I realized I had made a sensational shift. Ordinarily, feeling discouraged or depressed would have driven me to a bakery or a candy counter. Good for me!"

Perhaps the most important reward of all is simple self-acknowledgment, like LeShan's "Good for me!" I know that for myself, the acknowledgment "Hey, you finished that section," or "That's five chapters, now. You're almost halfway through" feels good. For runners, seeing the steady progression from half mile, to a mile, to two miles, to five miles can have a tremendously reinforcing effect.

Accomplishment is intrinsically rewarding when one is proceeding from a Driver-free standpoint, when there is no *Hurry Up*, *Be Perfect*, or *Try Hard* to ruin the feeling.

One way to discover unrecognized sources for rewarding yourself is to write a description of a perfect day. For the members in one group, a surprising similarity emerged in their typical "perfect" days. Getting up late, eating out, and having leisure time, free from the demands of housework or study, seemed most desired. The uniformity of their responses probably related to the homogeneity of this professional group, where most members were in their late twenties to their late fifties. For these busy people, the gift of free time was an extremely important form of self-nurturing.

Part of nurturing yourself involves expanding, through permission, the boundaries set by your Judge. Instead of confining your self-nurturing to eating out, for example, allow yourself a massage or a bouquet of flowers. Pay to have the house cleaned. Find a personal trainer or a therapist. What new rewards will you permit yourself to have?

Self-Assertion

Because so many conflicts can be resolved through self-assertion, it is important to develop your assertive skills to the highest degree possible. A thorough understanding of the principles of Self-Assertion is the fifth prerequisite of an effective Inner Guide. In *Self-Assertion for Women*, I discuss eight techniques that aid in the successful resolution of interpersonal difficulties. I will detail here the most important: (1) The "I" Message, (2) Muscle, and (3) Fogging:

"I" Messages

The skill to assert positive and negative feelings, to say no, and to initiate contact with others is necessary for an effective Guide. Learning to use "I" Messages, rather than "You" Messages, is a basic part of this skill. An "I" Message expresses a feeling or states an opinion. It communicates without blaming. On the other hand, a "You" Message resorts to the use of negative labels. "You" Messages judge another person. Contrast "You're insensitive." with "I get annoyed when you forget to introduce me to your friends." The future-oriented "I" Message, "Next time, I'd like you to introduce me to your friends," elicits an even better response.

The main strength of an "I" Message rests in two characteristics, high precision and low threat. An incident, described in one group, illustrates how "You" Messages fail in both of these regards. While in a public area, Shawn overheard two people talking. The first person began with the classic "You" Message, "You're wrong," which led immediately to the defensive reply, "Well, you're stupid." To quote Shawn, "It got worse from there." The interesting aspect of this interchange is that in the two or three minutes that Shawn listened, there was no mention of *who, what, where, why, or how.* In other words, very little actual information was relayed.

"You" Messages may be great vehicles for punishment, but they simply don't communicate very effectively. Moreover, "You" Messages provoke the person on the receiving end to strike back ("Well, you're stupid"), to withdraw ("Then there's no use talking to you"), or to become defensive ("I don't know about that").

In the "I" and "You" Messages that follow, examine your own reactions. Which do you prefer?

Situation 1: Jane's secretary neglects to write the time that a message arrived, information that Jane would like to have.

"You" Message: "You're not being careful enough in taking messages."

"I" Message: "I'd appreciate your making sure that the time is listed on each message."

Situation 2: Bob is annoyed to find Jill has made plans to get together with another couple without checking with him first.

"You" Message: "You're inconsiderate as hell. Don't you think I have any say in what we do?"

"I" Message: "Jill, I really feel annoyed when you make plans for me without asking me first."

Situation 3: Jenny comes home late from school, leaving the other members of her family without transportation.

"You" Message: "Don't you think of anyone but yourself? You're becoming totally insensitive to the rest of this family?"

"I" Message: "I don't want you to be late with the car again. I feel edgy wondering where you are and angry at being left hanging."

Situation 4: The waitress brings Don a meal he didn't order.

"You" Message: "You messed up my order."

"I" Message: "I think there's been a mistake. I ordered the eggplant, not the fettuccine."

Muscle

Most people assert themselves with more *Muscle* than is needed. As George Bach, one of the authors of *The Intimate Enemy,* described, "They drop the atomic bomb on Luxembourg". I can best show the importance of Muscle by sharing a story told to me by an acquaintance, Karen. After an exhausting trip, Karen flew back to San Francisco from the East Coast. On this five-hour flight, she planned to spend her time sleeping or, at the very most, reading a book. However, Karen sat next to someone who wanted to talk.

Rather than assert, "I've had such an exhausting trip that I don't feel much like talking today. I'm sure that another time I would have enjoyed chatting with you," Karen decided to hint, giving a one-word reply to each question from the other person. As with most hints, there was no effect, and as the flight progressed, Karen felt more and more irritated. Finally, she erupted, exclaiming, "I don't want to talk!"

Her traveling companion, who had been chatting merrily along, got a stricken look and said nothing more. However, rather than being pleased with the result of her expression, Karen felt guilty. She couldn't sleep, and she didn't feel like reading her book. Worse yet, she no longer had anyone with whom to talk. The net effect of the interchange between Karen and her fellow passenger was the lose-lose outcome that so often occurs with beginning assertive attempts.

Karen's assertion was an "I" Message. However, she had hit her traveling companion over the head with a club when a feather would have sufficed. Karen had simply used too much Muscle. Her difficulty came not from what she said, but from how she said it.

One of the most difficult assertive skills to master is the use of what I call Level One Muscle. Most people remain passive, come across aggressively, or use a very high level of Muscle in their communication. The effectiveness of the soft yet clear assertion that is Level One Muscle is completely neglected. If need be, there are higher levels that can be employed. Ironically, however, Level One Muscle is the most powerful because it prevents a power struggle. In other words, Level One Muscle is easy to respond to without a loss of face. Because of this, the other person tends also to respond positively, and a workable compromise is usually achieved.

Fogging

Fogging is a technique developed by Manuel Smith, in his book, *When I Say No I Feel Guilty*. Fogging prepares us to be an assertive receiver. All too often, other people send judgmental "You" Messages. Fogging allows you to walk past these negative messages without getting hooked by them.

When you Fog, you briefly acknowledge what has been said, without agreeing or disagreeing. By remaining neutral, you steer clear of the other person's judgments. You do not have to defend or acquiesce, nor do you get hooked into the other person's agenda. Instead, you remain free to reassert your own message. Thus, if Mark has decided to forego a business trip to

Europe because his feelings tell him that such a trip, great as it sounds, is unappealing at this time, he may have to contend with various judgmental comments from others. The responses that follow demonstrate two possible reactions to such comments, Fogging and Getting Hooked:

Judgmental Comment: Mark, you shouldn't miss this opportunity. You may never get another.
Fogging Response: That may be true, but I don't feel like making this one.
Hooked-In Response: Well, this isn't that good an opportunity. After all, I'd be working late. There wouldn't be much time for me to sightsee.

Judgmental Comment: Anyone in his right mind would go on a free trip to Europe.
Fogging Response: Although it may seem that way, I feel comfortable with my decision.
Hooked-In Response: What are you doing? Calling me crazy? What makes you think you know everything?

Judgmental Comment: Surely your wife doesn't mind your going?
Fogging Response: She may or may not mind, but I don't feel that the trip fits me right now.
Hooked-In Response: What makes you think that my wife controls me?

Judgmental Comment: I bet your boss is really upset that you're saying no to the trip.
Fogging Response: Well, she may be upset, but I have to make my decisions reflect what's best for me.
Hooked-In Response: Do you think so? Well, maybe I should go.

Judgmental Comment: You're being silly. You should go.
Fogging Response: Maybe so, but I'd rather sit this one out.
Hooked-In Response: I'd be silly if I go over there and have a miserable time. I don't like to travel alone.

Notice that Fogging allows Mark to maintain his own agenda without becoming defensive and without attacking the other person. The key words *may, sometimes,* and *seem* fulfill the requirement that Mark neither agree nor disagree with his opponent. For those of you who would like more information about these three assertive techniques, as well as others, I recommend my book, *Self-Assertion for Women.*

Summing Up

Over conversation one night a friend of mine, John, described how he had recently developed an Inner Guide for himself. He did this, however, only after an important learning experience.

"About a year ago," John explained, "I decided that yoga would be good for me. I set the goal of practicing the various yoga positions an hour each day, four days a week. The first week I accomplished my goal. The next week, I was busy and pressured with work deadlines, so I only got in three days. At that point, instead of just letting it go, I told myself that I would have to make up for the day I missed by practicing five days the coming week. Well, that week was busy also, and I again found time for only three days of exercise. At that point, I thought, 'Oh, to hell with it!'"

Several months later, John began experimenting with a new approach. After his negative experience with yoga, he consciously decided to reorient his Imposed Self away from arbitrary goals and judgments and to be more sensitive to his feelings. He shifted from Judge to Guide. In other words, John began functioning towards himself as a good parent or a good friend, allowing himself to make mistakes, to fail, in short to *Be Human*. John made this transition around another goal, running. This time, he gave himself permission *not* to run every day, *not* to go farther than he felt comfortable, *not* to compete with other joggers on the track.

"Sure, I sometimes feel competitive," continued John. "A guy passes me, and I have the urge to speed up. I admit to myself that it bothers me, but I also tell myself that it's okay to run at my own speed. I remind myself that I want my running to suit me.

You know something, I've been running now for six months, and I'm still enjoying it. I'm up to three miles a day, and I have no intention of stopping."

The bottom line is this: your Inner Guide works. When you objectively consider your environment and your feelings, when you utilize the principles of small steps and ample rewards, and when you operate within an assertive framework, you maximize your positive feelings. In doing so, you increase your ability to fulfill your own potential. Contrasted to the empty orders of your Judge, your Inner Guide offers you a positive plan of action, replacing a tension-filled tightrope with a workable pathway to success.

CHAPTER 8

Overcoming the Obstacles to Self Support

Let's say you have begun replacing your negative tapes with positive ones. Hooray for you! You are escaping from an abusive inner companion. Only, beware. Like any prisoner nearing freedom, you will find guards who suddenly appear and attempt to block your exit.

The Second Line of Defense

Having cracked the rigid structure by which you have lived your life, you now confront the obstacles, warnings and criticisms of the Imposed Self as never before. Each brick of the Judgmental wall now hits you on the head with its critical sting, "You'll be sorry.", tempting you to make a hasty retreat to the old position. However, if you continue forward, these bricks will soon be at your feet. Thus, when Sally refuses to rescue her friend by trying to solve her problems, she finds herself immersed in a fearful preoccupation "What will happen now?" She has nagging doubts that she is "insensitive" or "selfish." Likewise, when Bob relaxes outdoors in the lounge chair, he suddenly faces every judgment that has prevented him from relaxing ("You're lazy. You're nonproductive. Why aren't you doing something?").

By seeing these old messages as the bricks holding up the old judgmental structure, you can allow them to fall by the wayside. Even if you listen to them again and return to your old behavior, you will do so with an added ingredient of awareness. Although Sally found herself occasionally rescuing someone and going against her own feelings, she now was exquisitely aware of the cost of this and aware that she had a choice. Even if she repeats this process many more times, Sally will continue to build her inner conviction that she must operate in her own behalf.

New attitudes and self-messages also provoke the Second Line of Defense. When Lisa, a woman with the belief "I'm unattractive," first acknowledged to herself that many men actually seemed to like her and that one man in particular appeared quite taken with her, she immediately retreated, saying, "Oh, I'm just selling myself a bill of goods. This attention doesn't mean a thing. I'm being foolish to think otherwise. I can't take the risk."

Lisa's Self-Affirmation provoked a host of negative self-labels. She was "foolish" to feel positive and only "selling herself a bill of goods." The attention from her male friend was "meaningless." Lisa's positive affirmation also elicited the catastrophic thought, "If you let yourself believe this heady stuff, you're going to be hurt and disappointed." The anxiety created by this negative barrage effectively blocked Lisa's escape from her depressing belief "I'm not attractive."

Our culture has no shortage of Stoppers that work against self-support. Labels like "conceited" and "immodest" punish our Self-Affirmations. We pride ourselves on being too "realistic" or "intellectually honest" to accept and enjoy positive information. We give "luck" the credit for any positive achievement ("It was sure a lucky break that I was hired for my new job"). Negative occurrences rest, of course, solely upon our own backs. We fail to give them comparable, critical scrutiny.

Combating the Second Line of Defense takes almost as much work as repudiating the first. The process, however, is the same. The negative labels and catastrophes that punish your new self-message must be challenged. The questions "What am I telling myself?" "Is this helpful?" and so on, allow you to walk past these second obstacles just as you negotiated the first. The examples that follow spotlight the operation of the Second Line of Defense and suggest the supportive alternatives that can neutralize its influence.

Consider a positive self-message that you wish to assert, or a Permission you want to give yourself. Be aware of any "second thoughts" that undermine your supportive self-talk, as you do. The following examples illustrate how to do this.

Example 1:

Self-Support: "I don't like this area of study. I've given it a fair chance and my feelings tell me that it doesn't fit. It's okay for me to let it go and explore something new."

Second Line of Defense: "Nice try. You're just lazy. You don't want to do any work. You never finish anything. You're a quitter."

Supportive Alternative: "Wait a minute. I tried out that area and didn't like it. I haven't quit anything. I've learned something about myself and can now move on to explore other alternatives. I'm not putting a time limit on myself."

Example 2:

Self-Support: "It's okay to consider myself a competent writer, whether or not I get the grant I've applied for."

Second Line of Defense: "It's the bottom line that counts."

Supportive Alternative: "No. My self-worth doesn't have to rest on the opinion of others. There are many reasons why grants aren't awarded. These days only one person in ten is funded. I will not buy the bottom-line notion when it relates to my own self-worth."

Example 3:

Self-Support: "I met someone at the ballet yesterday who wants to get together with me again. I guess I'm more attractive than I thought".

Second Line of Defense: "Oh that was just a line. He'll never call."

Supportive Alternative: "Wait. I don't know that. Even if it doesn't work out, I liked the conversation and the attention. I'm going to enjoy the feeling and let it soak in.

Example 4:

Self-Support: "There were a lot of positive things that I did for my husband. I wasn't a complete failure as a wife."

Second Line of Defense: "Those things were trivial. They don't count."

Supportive Alternative: "Just a minute. It's okay for me to acknowledge the positive. I'm going to be fair to myself, just as I would be to another person."

Driver Interference

Sometimes, the Second Line of Defense attempts to place the new wine of your supportive self talk into the old casks and bottles of the judgmental framework. The Drivers, *Be Perfect, Hurry Up, Please Others, Be Strong,* and *Try Hard,* undermine you when your beginning attempts at being supportive are not perfect or when your negative self-talk does not go away quickly.

When Liz began telling me all the supportive things that she had done for herself the previous week, she seemed quite excited. However, she also related that she felt very stressed.

I asked Liz to imagine herself sitting in the empty chair in front of her and to show both of us how she had been stressing Liz. Slowly she began to formulate the negative message: "You aren't going fast enough. There are still times when you know what to do, and you don't do it. You've got to try harder." She immediately saw one primary source of her stress. The three Drivers, *Hurry Up*, *Be Perfect*, and *Try Hard*, had taken control and were contaminating her new decision to support herself. Even though these Drivers were operating like a stealth missile, underneath her radar of consciousness, they were exerting a major toxic effect, dragging down her energy and enthusiasm.

As Liz moved into the empty chair, she answered back, "Let me go at my own pace. All this pressure is tiring me out. I'll get there, just leave me alone." As an aside, Liz said to me, "That's my mother. Nothing I ever did was enough to please her."

It is very easy for the decision to support yourself to be hijacked by an old judgmental habit. The judgmental and the growth frameworks are incompatible. We cannot serve them both. The Intrinsic Self requires nothing less than complete respect and trust.

False Pride

A final obstacle to the development of self-support is what analyst Karen Horney refers to as "False Pride." We refuse to let go of the demands and expectations of the Imposed Self because these expectations alone seem capable of rescuing us from our own self-hate. Horney describes how early circumstances turn us away from our genuine desires and potentials toward a grim determination to become an ideal person, one who is famous, successful, wealthy, or acclaimed. The extent to which we feel worthless, inadequate, and unloved gives us some measure of our need to recreate ourselves into an ideal image.

The basic belief here is "If only I can become, accomplish, or achieve such and such, then I will be okay." This can vary from getting a Ph.D. to making $500,000 a year, from marrying a wealthy man, to being in the "right" social group. Unfortunately, individuals who base their self-worth on externals never quite make it. Something always falls short. The problem is that pride or self esteem based on such externals alone is not in the service of the Intrinsic Self. Keeping up with the "right" social group is likely to be boring and stressful. Making $500,000 a year may cost you your health and end in a life of isolation or a premature death.

The tenacity of False Pride also derives from the conviction that the standards of the Imposed Self should be upheld and that you will be rewarded if they are and punished if they are not. We tell ourselves that if we *Try Hard* enough, it is indeed possible to become the ideal person we desire to be. Then other people will be sorry. Life will treat us differently. Any suggestion that the requirements of the Imposed Self are impossible to attain is met with rage: "I should be above needing anyone, and I will be!" or "I must accomplish something important! The things that I'm doing now aren't enough!" Ian Fleming created in James Bond an illusory ideal that millions have modeled their lives after. The current dark heroes of video games present to vulnerable isolates the chance to control this world with total power and no limitations. This never to be attained fantasy propels avoidance of the real world of struggle, rejection, and limited successes.

For those trapped in the judgmental model, fantasy seems the only means of escape. Yet, the answer is simple, unless you let go of the desire to recreate yourself in an ideal image, you can never appreciate or love or respect the person you really are. To say to yourself, "That was a job well done," will not be possible, because something about the job will inevitably fall short of your Imposed Self's standards. The observation, "I was really successful today", will be dampened by the concern, "Can I do it again tomorrow?" Genuine growth steps will be snubbed with the comment "Everyone else has already done that." In fact, you will never win the judgmental prize of omnipotence, omniscience, or perfect love. As we know, "the Perfect is the enemy of the Good." In the end, the quest for perfection will destroy the good in your life.

CHAPTER 9

Sex and Self-Talk

Will I get an erection?
Can I keep it?
Am I going to be able to satisfy my partner?
Will I have an orgasm?
Do I want to have sex?
Will my partner get mad if I don't?
Is there something wrong with me?
Am I normal?

The same critical focus that permeates every other aspect of your life may affect your sexuality as well. Displeased with your natural response, you may push for better, longer-lasting, more intense reactions, paradoxically interfering with your inherent sexual capacity. Chasing the elusive butterfly of perfection, you destroy the very experience you desire to create. An incredible burden (you *should* do this and *don't* do that) sits upon this natural function.

Sex and Internal Commands

According to Masters and Johnson, the greatest known deterrent to effective sexual functioning is performance anxiety. *Be Perfect, Hurry Up, Be Strong, Please Others*, and *Try Hard* commands generate this anxiety. With these Drivers in operation, a sexual relationship becomes a proving ground for an individual's masculinity or femininity. It can even become the final measure of self-worth. Is there any surprise that little room is left for feelings of arousal and desire?

The Driver that stands out in its capacity to undermine sexual arousal is the demand to *Be Perfect*. The *Be Perfect* Driver may require that sexual contact always involve intercourse. ("What's wrong with me? Why can't

I make it?") It may demand an orgasm one hundred percent of the time. ("Did you? Why not? Did I do something wrong?") There may even be the expectation of simultaneous or multiple orgasms. ("Why couldn't I last longer? I'm depriving you.") Sex becomes an achievement to be met or an obstacle to be overcome.

Not only does the intrusive self-talk generated by *Be Perfect* focus on an individual's own sexuality; it can also spotlight a partner's imperfections. Bill wants Sara to have an orgasm with each sexual encounter. When she doesn't, he feels inadequate and gets mad at himself, and mad at her. Yet the more Sara tries to "achieve" orgasm, knowing that Bill is working hard to give her one, the more frustrating and difficult it becomes.

Sara's self-talk gives some sense of her inner turmoil: "Am I going to get aroused? What's wrong with me? Why do I have to have this problem? It's hopeless. I'll never be able to come. Maybe I should just fake it. Bill's trying hard. I shouldn't make him feel bad." The anxiety generated by Sara's own self-talk makes it impossible to relax and tune into her own sexual feelings. Instead, she becomes a spectator, monitoring her own degree of arousal.

Correspondingly, Bill's self talk is also critical of Sara. Because he tends to externalize, he focuses blame outwardly. "Goddamn it. What's wrong with Sara? Why do I have a girlfriend who's frigid? I deserve better than this. I'm doing everything right." For Sara, the combination of Bill's pressure and her own, creates a negative internal environment where sexual arousal cannot occur.

Although triggered by Bill's *Be Perfect* Claim, Sara's own Drivers, Stoppers, and Confusers rest upon the *Please Others* messages in her inner speech constellation. She would be less affected by Bill's *Be Perfect* ideal and freer to speak up for herself, if she were not basing her own self-worth on pleasing him.

Are you like Sara? In trying to please your partner, do you dampen your own sexual enjoyment? Most commonly, a woman tries to hurry up her sexual response, while a man struggles to slow his down. Each attempt, well intentioned though it may be, exacerbates rather than resolves the arousal problem. A vicious downward spiral is established, where anxiety leads to nonperformance, which leads to even more anxiety.

A standard prescription of most sex therapy is to forbid sexual intercourse to a dysfunctional couple. The sensate focus exercises developed by Masters and Johnson actually go so far as to forbid any genital stimulation during initial touch sessions. By removing the couple's focus from success or achievement or the endpoint goal of orgasm, an opportunity for a leisurely, non-demand pleasuring is provided. Thus, the power of the *Be Perfect* Driver is reduced.

The structure of pleasuring exercises (one person gives while the other receives) aids in turning off the *Hurry Up, Try Hard,* and *Please Others* Drivers as well. Some programs assign a time period (twenty minutes, for example) for non-genital pleasuring. In the beginning, this time interval may seem extraordinarily long for two people, who both have incessant *Hurry Up* demands. Yet, as Masters and Johnson note in *Human Sexuality Inadequacy,* "For most women, and for many men, the sensate focus sessions represent the first opportunity they have ever had to 'think and feel' sensuously and at leisure without intrusion upon the experience by the demand for endpoint release (own or partner's), without the need to explain their sensate preferences, without the demand for personal reassurance, or without a sense of need to 'return the favor.'"

Such "new permissions", existing within the therapy process, are necessary to break the stranglehold of the judgmental *should sys*tem. As we have seen repeatedly, this system has little relevance to reality, having been passed on in the context of shame, bravado, and fear. The damage of this misdirection is noted in *Male Sexuality,* where Bernie Zilbergeld describes how basically normal, healthy men "rigidly cling to certain rules as to how sex should be and how a man should act in sex." Zilbergeld states that men have "unrealistic and, in fact, superhuman standards by which to measure their equipment, performance, and satisfaction, thus insuring a perpetual no-win situation. Whatever men do, when compared to the standards they learned, it's somehow not enough."

For men, abiding by the judgmental position has meant a continuation of the *Be Perfect, Be Strong* achievement demands that are part of the traditional masculine role in other areas. Stopper labels like "weak, inept, and un-masculine" have kept at bay any soft feelings that might spontaneously arise. The myths that Bernie Zilbergeld describes in *Male Sexuality* highlight the judgmental position's influence on the sexual behavior of men. These myths include a large number of Drivers, Stoppers, and Confusers:

MYTH 1: Men should not have, or at least not express, certain feelings: feelings of weakness, confusion, fear, vulnerability, tenderness, compassion, and sensuality.

The Driver involved is, of course, that old bastion of the masculine role, *Be Strong.* If you doubt this, consider the question I asked one class. "Can you imagine any macho movie hero suggesting to his costar, 'I need to be held,' or 'Let's cuddle'?" The very word "cuddle" seems incongruous with the traditional masculine image. Yet the need for touch, for affection, and for nurturing is an important *human* need. Naturally, this *Be Strong* Driver leaves many women feeling deprived. Women complain that they do not get enough touching, hugging, and caressing. All too often, men consider touch as a prelude to sexual intercourse, not important in and of itself.

MYTH 2: In sex, as elsewhere, it's performance that counts.

Here again, sex is seen in terms of achievement, rather than pleasure. The Drivers *Try Hard* and *Be Perfect* turn sex into work. I can still remember the instruction of one sex therapist to a male client who was very concerned with the performance issues of how often and for how long: "Let's focus on your becoming less of a bookkeeper and more of a lover."

MYTH 3: The man must take charge and orchestrate sex.

According to this myth, there is no room for a man to be passive, only the demand to *Try Hard* and *Be Strong*. Again, sex is work. Having to remain in control, the man is deprived of the opportunity to be taken care of and nurtured. Of course, the female partner is also denied. If the man is always to be in charge, she in turn must always be on *his* sexual agenda. Her own assertion is not permitted. Is there any doubt that power struggles develop over this inflexible rule?

MYTH 4: A man always wants and is always ready to have sex.

The Drivers are *Be Perfect* and *Be Strong*. This myth ignores the great number of external and internal factors that can and do influence human sexual arousal. Many cases of impotence derive from this belief and one negative experience. Normally, such an experience is based on nothing more than the fact that the necessary conditions for sexual arousal were not met. These conditions for men and for women generally include an interested and interesting partner, a safe setting, an atmosphere of acceptance, and a freedom from external preoccupations and worries. The *Be Perfect* tightrope does not allow a man to assert, "I don't feel like sex tonight," "I've had too much to eat and drink," or "I'd rather just be close."

MYTH 5: All physical contact must lead to sex.

MYTH 6: Sex equals intercourse.

MYTH 7: Sex requires an erection.

MYTH 8: Good sex is a linear progression of increased excitement terminated only by orgasm.

Myths 5, 6, 7, and 8 are all based on the *Be Perfect* Driver in conjunction with the familiar correlate of Either/Or Thinking. Sex is defined as one hundred percent sexual intercourse (or for some, one hundred percent simultaneous orgasm through intercourse). Anything else constitutes a failure. The term "foreplay," meaning *what comes before,* is an interesting by-product of these myths. It reinforces the idea that any sexual activity other than intercourse is incomplete.

Men are so concerned about completing the obstacle course that culminates in sexual intercourse that they do not realize that many women value communication and warmth over performance. For most women, a penis in the vagina is not the only, or necessarily the optimal, means of achieving sexual satisfaction. A man does not have to have an erection to arouse his partner. Yet, within the judgmental structure, the absence of an erection means no sex.

Women collude in this myth. In Lillian Rubin's *Women of a Certain Age: The Midlife Search for Self,* several women admitted holding back their own emerging mid-life sexuality out of the fear that their husbands could not meet their needs. In each case, sex was defined solely as sexual intercourse. These women were walking on eggs around their partners' inability to get or to maintain an erection. Yet with such a demand placed upon an involuntary function, it is no wonder that sexual avoidance and impotence occur.

Women have incorporated equally damaging myths and self talk. For them, the *Please Others* Driver has dominated, leading to a focus on male pleasure and satisfaction at the expense of their own. Labels like "castrating" and "pushy" have effectively squelched the more assertive, demanding aspects of female sexuality. One female myth holds that a woman should be able to have an orgasm through sexual intercourse alone. As in most situations, what we have been taught *should* be is not necessarily what is. Lonnie Garfield Barbach in her book *For Yourself* corrects this myth: "The physiological fact is that intercourse alone just doesn't seem to provide enough of the right kind of stimulation to the right area to permit many women to become aroused to the point of orgasm."

So, too, the myth that a woman must have sex based on her partner's need rather than upon her own has had a negative influence. The Driver *Please Others* pushes many women to override their own feelings and submit to the demands of their partners. Fear of rejection or a concern that they will be seen as prudes, teases, or frigid leads many women, especially very young women, into sexual activity before they are ready for it.

Along these same lines, Barbach notes the erroneous belief held by many that "sex is not as necessary for women as it is for men" and that "a man's sexual release is more important than a woman's." Here, a woman overvalues her partner's sexual feelings and undervalues her own.

Sex and Stoppers

Existing, side by side with the push toward ever more intense sexual performance, are a number of strong prohibitions against sexual enjoyment. Years of messages say *don't*: *don't* enjoy; *don't* be sexual; *don't* initiate; *don't* communicate; *don't* show your feelings; *don't* be vulnerable. Needless to say, the negative self-talk deriving from these messages interferes with sexual arousal. There are two primary areas where this Stopper intrusion occurs: (1) in Sexual Assertion and (2) in the Appreciation of One's Own Sexuality.

Sex and Self-Assertion

If Stoppers interfere with assertion in general, they are present to an even greater degree when it comes to sexual communication. Fears of rejection, criticism, and disapproval increase as the degree of sexual intimacy increases. Yet if you are not free to share your feelings, especially questioning and anxious feelings, during sex, they stay with you, growing larger, even as you fight to push them aside. Unexpressed, these negative and anxious feelings become obstacles to sexual arousal.

Therapists Bernard Apfelbaum and Martin Williams of the Berkeley Sex Therapy Group help people voice the feelings that arise during a sexual encounter, especially feelings that differ from society's "this is all so wonderful" ideal. In therapy, a set of "script lines" is developed with each individual to describe the emotions experienced during a specific sexual encounter. Once articulated, they are written down so that when similar feelings arise again, they can be voiced.

Within the protective framework of sexual therapy, people often find that the honest assertion of heretofore unspoken feelings can lead to an intimacy and subsequent arousal impossible to attain when energy is spent trying to deny negative emotions and capture a perfect sexual interlude.

Statements like "I'm feeling really hopeless about ever getting turned on", or "I'm embarrassed," make room for closeness and arousal where distance and alienation have been before. In a therapy context, an environment is created where this negative expression can be viewed as a positive desire for intimacy rather than as an attack or as a punishment. Listed below are some of the "script lines" that the Berkeley Sex Therapy Group has employed in working with sexual difficulties. Notice the level of intimacy involved in these assertions. Notice further how they go beyond our standard notions of what should be communicated during sex:

> I'm wondering how you're feeling.
> I feel out of touch, cut off from my body.
> I feel alone.
> I wish you could help me to get out of this mold.
> I feel embarrassed.
> These feelings seem so irrational. They're almost ridiculous.
> I'm afraid that I will do something wrong.
> I'm afraid you might be bored.
> I feel like I've got to do something.
> I'm worried that you might be getting impatient.
> I want to touch you while you're stroking me.
> I feel so desperate.

When negative feelings can be asserted at the exact moment they are experienced, a communication occurs, which increases intimacy and gives immediate feedback. Naturally, this kind of assertion requires overriding the rigid requirement against interrupting one's partner. Thus, if Maureen is feeling left out as Charles is moving to higher levels of excitement, it is important that she voice her sense of isolation at that moment, not later over dinner, when there is nothing that can be done to alter her feelings of estrangement.

It is not uncommon for two people to be at one level sexually and at another level emotionally. In our society, sexual barriers are often penetrated more easily than emotional ones. A woman who has spent the night with a man may feel awkward about telephoning him the next day. The standard Stoppers: Catastrophizing ("Maybe he doesn't like me"), Negative Self-Labels ("I don't want to seem pushy"), or Rigid Requirements ("I'll call *if* he has indicated that he wants to see me again"), can inhibit even minimum assertion.

A woman in this position finds herself at a superficial level emotionally, while at a very intimate level sexually.

Even committed couples allow that intimate communication is nonexistent where sex is concerned. The fact that so many women (and men) fake orgasm is one indication that intimate assertion is blocked. *The Hite Report* found that over a third of the women responding answered yes to lying about orgasm. Bernie Zilbergeld explains male faking in this way, "They can't fake erections, but we know of more than a few who fake orgasms. But the main things they fake are their feelings. They pretend to be confident when they're not; to know when they don't; to be comfortable when they're uneasy; to be interested when they couldn't care less; and to enjoy when they feel otherwise."

Such deception, whether it involves orgasms or feelings, is motivated by many *shoulds* and *don'ts*: by the desire to avoid punishment or rejection; by the need to please; by the fear of hurting one's partner's feelings; or by the hope of getting the sexual encounter over with more quickly. Of course, the false information conveyed by these deceptions leads the partner to assume that everything is okay. This decreases the chance of achieving the conditions necessary for adequate arousal. Many of the pleasuring exercises that form the basis of sex therapy provide a framework that says, "It's okay to be honest. It's okay to communicate your likes and dislikes. It's okay to assert your feelings. It's okay not to know everything." The need for such an explicit mechanism to exist in order for such basic permissions to be felt is testimony to the strength of the judgmental position.

The Appreciation of Your Own Sexuality

The appreciation of your own body and the acceptance of yourself as a sexual being is a crucial ingredient of sexual arousal. Because of the conditioning of prior negative experiences, you may have little delight in your body. The picture-perfect Playboy centerfold and the media image of the sexual stud may have sharpened your *Be Perfect* focus to a highly critical edge. Anxiety/punishment tapes, with their negative labels and catastrophes, may be ever-present. Lynette, for example, considered herself as no longer a "real" woman after her menopause. She viewed her sexual self as "incomplete." When she realized the negative viewpoint that she was bringing to every sexual encounter, she chose to let go of these negative labels. She also found herself orgasmic again for the first time in several years.

In *For Yourself,* one of the first exercises that Barbach suggests for the pre-orgasmic woman is the examining of her body in front of a full-length mirror. Then, she is encouraged to explore her body with her hands. These first steps form the beginning of a detailed program whose purpose is to make the woman and her partner knowledgeable about and comfortable with her individual sexual response.

This same kind of permission is important for men as well. While men have generally had fewer sexual roadblocks, they have frequently had *more* sensual ones. Consider, for example, how many men would feel comfortable about taking a bubble bath or sleeping on satin sheets. Again, it frequently takes an authoritative program to give such permission. The Masters and Johnson sensate focus exercises clearly assert that it's okay to enjoy and spend time on non-genital pleasure. It is, in fact, a demand of their program. This is a new experience to the man for whom touch has simply been a signal to rush into sexual intercourse. Of course, this kind of sensual focus and permission enhances rather than replaces sexual arousal.

The Freedom to Say "No"

The ability to say "No" to unwanted sexual activity is a necessary prerequisite to being able to say "Yes" to sex in a genuinely free way. The pressure to be sexually active is occurring at younger and younger ages, as the social constraints that empower someone to say "No" are lessening. Those unwilling to experiment sexually are labeled as "prudes". Young clients of mine fear social ostracism if they are not sexually intimate, quickly. This is a dramatic contrast to the experience of the prior generation, who faced labels, "loose" or "cheap", even if the couple were in a committed relationship.

The costs of too early and too much has been damaging, not only to young women, but to young men as well. We have become a "tissue paper culture". Instant use followed by instant discard. A callous view of others is one consequence of this false intimacy and gratification.

The ability to listen to and trust your own deepest intuition is crucial. You must learn to understand the difference between authentic feelings and mere impulse reactions, however strong these may be. The feelings that emanate from the Intrinsic Self support the creation of a protective and nurturing environment for the unfolding of sexual intimacy. Being intoxicated on drugs or alcohol can lead only to the self-destructive loss of impulse control. A simple question may help here: "Is my adult self or my child self driving the car?" Being drunk or high will definitely hand the emotional keys over to the child. The usual result is an emotional car crash. Sleeping with a stranger may provide a sense of momentary adventure, but it is a short road to tragedy. Your Inner Guide must function as a protective parent to your inner child.

Using the Five- Step Method

In the following examples, the Five-Step Method is applied to three common sexual concerns: (1) the Pressure for Orgasm, (2) Performance Anxiety, and (3) the Fear of Saying "No."

Dealing with External Pressure:

Sara feels pressured by Bill to have an orgasm. In her desire to meet his expectations, she finds her own sexual arousal decreasing. Sara goes through the five-step process as a way of clarifying her feelings:

STEP 1: "What am I telling myself?"

"I'm saying that something is wrong with me. Bill is only trying to help. I can't say anything negative to him. I don't want him to feel bad. I'll just try harder."

STEP 2: "Is my self-talk helpful?"

"Well, I guess not. I'm feeling tense, and Bill seems to be getting even more upset with me. I could fake an orgasm, but I've never done that with Bill before. I don't want to do that. Maybe I don't have to view what is happening as entirely my fault. I felt okay about my response before Bill got so upset."

STEP 3: "Is there a Driver, Stopper, or Confuser in operation?"

"I'm trying hard to please Bill. He's trying hard to please me. I'd feel better if there wasn't so much fuss about my having an orgasm."

STEP 4: "What Permission and Self-Affirmation can I use?"

"I can say that it's okay for me to stop taking care of Bill's feelings and to tell him what I want. It's okay for me to stop trying to have an orgasm and let it happen."

STEP 5: "What kind of action can I take?"

"Well, first, I'll talk to Bill. I'll see how he reacts. If there's still a problem between us, then perhaps we need to consult a sex therapist."

Confronting Performance Anxiety:

Michael is very anxious about his ability to perform sexually. Because of his concern, he has withdrawn from almost all interaction with women.

STEP 1: "What am I telling myself?"

"I'm saying that I can't let on that I am anxious about getting an erection, because if I do, the woman I'm with will reject me. I'm saying that I won't date anyone until I can get over this problem. I'm saying that I'm not much of a man."

STEP 2: "Is my Self-Talk helping?"

"Well, I'm isolated and depressed and feel like hell. I still can't get it up. I guess it isn't helping much."

STEP 3: "What are the Drivers, Stoppers, or Confusers in operation?"

"Be Strong. I don't want to have any problems, especially sexual ones. I guess I'm catastrophizing that a woman wouldn't understand, and I haven't even shared my feelings with a woman. I'm labeling myself 'not a man'."

STEP 4: "What Permission or Self-Affirmation will I give myself?"

"I can tell myself that it's okay to have feelings and to express them. My feelings are there whether I like them or not. Maybe a woman will like me even if I'm not great in bed. Hell, maybe if I weren't keeping all this junk to myself, I could function. I'm in therapy. Maybe a woman would be willing to work with me."

STEP 5: "What action can I take?"

"I think I'll let myself start dating, and forget about having intercourse for a while. If I meet someone I really like, I'll tell her what my problem is and see how she reacts. It's not hopeless. I've simply got to stop pressuring myself and let myself do what I feel like doing, even if it's nothing."

Resisting Sexual Demands:

Emmy has gone out on a date with Jeremy. She really likes him and wants to get to know him. Jeremy asks Emmy if she wants to go back to his apartment. Emmy is beginning to feel uncomfortable. She doesn't know what Jeremy expects but is afraid he'll either reject her or think she's being presumptuous if she brings up her concerns. Emmy quickly asks herself:

STEP 1: "What am I telling myself?"

"I'm telling myself that I will look stupid if I bring up what I'm feeling. He'll think I'm blaming him, when he hasn't done anything."

STEP 2: "Is my Self-Talk helping?"

"No. I'm feeling sick at my stomach."

STEP 3: "What's the Driver, Stopper, or Confuser?"

"I'm catastrophizing that if I assert my concerns, everything will blow up. I'm calling myself stupid, a negative self- label. I'm assuming he'll react negatively."

STEP 4: "What Permission or Self Affirmation will I give myself?"

"It's okay to express my feelings. I'm simply checking things out, not accusing. If he's the kind of man I want, he'll respond positively. If not, it's best I know sooner rather than later."

STEP 5: "What action will I take?"

"I'll say to Jeremy, 'I'm feeling a bit uncomfortable, because I'm not clear what your expectations are if we go to your apartment.' Then, I'll see what he says and go from there."

Now examine your own negative self-talk concerning sex. Are you in the judgmental or in the growth position?

JUDGMENTAL POSITION: Sex must have a goal: tension reduction, procreation, or the affirmation of sexual prowess. Therefore, sex should always result in intercourse and orgasm.
GROWTH POSITION: Sexual feelings are valid experiences in and of themselves. They don't have to lead to anything to be enjoyed.

JUDGMENTAL POSITION: A sexual experience shouldn't cause negative feelings. If it does, don't let on. Suppress feelings of loneliness, sadness, or vulnerability.
GROWTH POSITION: Unless you are free to accept and express whatever you feel, a sexual encounter becomes an alienating rather than a nurturing experience.

JUDGMENTAL POSITION: You should be able to put aside any problems and become aroused regardless of what's going on within your relationship.

GROWTH POSITION: For some people, bypassing problems is not possible. Sexual feelings do not exist in isolation.

JUDGMENTAL POSITION: You should know in advance whether or not you're interested in sexual intercourse, so that you don't mislead your partner. Be sure you want to go the full distance before you buy your ticket.

GROWTH POSITION: It's okay to honor your feelings and refuse to push them aside. It's okay to let your experience determine whether you want to stop or continue. You are not on a train to a particular destination. You're expressing yourself sexually with another person.

JUDGMENTAL POSITION: You should always be ready for sex and always be able to perform.

GROWTH POSITION: Both men and women have the right to say "no". Sex involves communication. It's okay to express your feelings during sex.

JUDGMENTAL POSITION: You should not need to tell your partner what pleases you. Likewise, you should know the "right" way to please your partner.

GROWTH POSITION: Communication of likes and dislikes is essential for both men and women. There is no "right" way. People differ in what is pleasuring to them. This changes on a day-by-day, even moment-by-moment basis. It is essential to remember that you are the *only* expert about your sexuality.

CHAPTER 10

Talking Yourself into Anger

An old story tells about a man, driving through the countryside, who has a flat tire. He realizes to his chagrin that he cannot repair the tire because he doesn't have a jack. However, having just passed a farmhouse, he confidently assures himself, "No sweat. I'm sure the people living in that farmhouse will be happy to lend me a jack." With that thought, he starts walking.

After going a short distance, the traveler begins to reconsider. "I wonder just how generous those people are going to be. After all, I'm at their mercy. I've got to have a jack, and no one else is around." After walking a bit further, he adds, "I'll bet that jack is going to cost me a pretty penny. I'm a stranger here. They'll certainly try to get every bit of mileage that they can from my problem." As he approaches the house and knocks on the door, he makes his final assumption, "I bet they're going to rip me off!"

About this time, a man leans out of the upper window and, in a not unfriendly voice asks, "What can I do for you, stranger?"

"Not a damn thing," the traveler angrily replies. "I wouldn't take any help from you if my life depended on it."

This joke's humor, of course, lies in the farmer's innocence in provoking the attack. The traveler's anger springs totally from his own internal dialogue. The realization that this curious process is far from unusual allows us to laugh not only at the traveler but at ourselves as well. It illustrates how anger, just like depression, is often self-generated. Although anger feels better than depression, it is not an emotion to cultivate.

Friedman and Rosenman, the authors of *Type A Behavior and Your Heart,* describes how anger results in a massive physiological preparation for action: "If you become intensely angered by some phenomenon, your hypothalamus will almost instantaneously send signals to all or almost all the nerve endings of your sympathetic nervous system (that portion of your nervous system not directly under your control), causing them to secrete relatively large amounts of epinephrine and norepinephrine. In addition, this same fit of anger will probably also induce the hypothalamus to send additional messages to the pituitary gland, the master of all endocrine glands, urging it to discharge some of its own exclusively manufactured hormones (such as growth hormone) and also to send out chemical signals to the adrenal, sex, and thyroid glands and the pancreas as well, so that they in turn may secrete excess amounts of their exclusively manufactured hormones." When anger is a *chronic* occurrence, it is associated with coronary heart disease. Interestingly, such anger often derives from Drivers, Stoppers, and Confusers.

Driver-Generated Anger

Analyst Karen Horney employed the term "Neurotic Claims" to describe one anger-generating mechanism. A Claim is a *"should"* placed on someone else. You can apply demands like *Hurry Up, Be Perfect, Be Strong, Please Others*, and *Try Hard* to other people as well as to yourself. Those of you who externalize blame are very much inclined to put Claims onto other people. The use of Claims resonates with the question that Jesus asked in the Sermon on the Mount: "Why do you see the speck that is in your brother's eye, but do not notice the log that is in your own?"

Quite often, the severest Claims are placed on those closest to you. This is because your husband, wife, or children are the people you most view as extensions of yourself. Because you believe that their behaviors reflect upon you, you apply your own *"should's"* to them. Paradoxically, the critical eye cast upon close relations and friends by the Judge often lead you to treat those you love far worse than you would treat anyone else.

Role-related Claims ("You're my wife, and I expect you to act that way." or "I don't want any child of mine wearing his hair like that.")" rest on this tendency to incorporate those close to you into your own judgmental system. Critically overseeing the behavior of an intimate, whether it is due to marital expectations or to the outward projection of an internal "should" system, can ultimately lead to the destruction of the relationship. For example, a *Be Perfect* Claim applied to one's partner will result in constant faultfinding. "Why did you tell me you were going to be home all day? When I called, you weren't." or "You shouldn't have bought that kind of salad oil. You're wasting money."

Such statements rest upon a mountain of righteous indignation. The Judgmental Claim, "You should *Be Perfect*", translates, "You should do everything the way I want it done." The outstanding characteristic of a Claim is the small tolerance or room for error it gives another person. The recipient of a Claim is expected to walk the familiar tightrope. There is no room for changes in plans, for spontaneity, or even for simple feelings.

After a time, the victim of such inordinate demands may rebel, break the too-tight leash, fight back, or even leave the relationship. Or, the victim may simply acquiesce, giving up the freedom to operate by the signals of his own Intrinsic Self. This last solution occurs only amid great inner turmoil. The Intrinsic Self is never deserted without protest. Yet, without assistance, many people fail to extricate themselves from the destructive Claims of others.

Why accept the Claims of another person? Doesn't each individual have the external freedom not to accept them? This issue is not as simple or as straightforward as it might seem. For example, many people feel trapped within their marriages for economic reasons. To fight against a husband's Claims is also to combat the fear of divorce and the very real possibility of a marginal economic existence. For a man to challenge a wife's demands may generate turmoil within the family and impact the life of his children.

Ultimately, you buy into the Claims of another person because that person's rigid demands are not all that different from the messages of your own Imposed Self. If you *internalize*, you will be willing to accept the blame placed on you by someone who *externalizes*. You will swallow whole any criticism without regard to its factual base. The strength of your own internal Drivers actually provides a good measure of your vulnerability to the Claims of others. In therapy, a good measure of a client's progress can be found in her ability to evaluate critically the negative judgments of others. As Clarissa revealed, "I no longer soak up everything James says to me. I don't see him as the ultimate authority anymore. Consequently, I don't feel as bad during our arguments."

Claims, of course, can be placed upon strangers, business associates, public figures, and as Horney notes, even upon life itself. They are not confined to family members or intimate relationships. Your expectations of the world can lead to anger and disappointment.

The idea that everything should go your way is one such expectation. When the toast burns, the operator cuts off your call, or you miss the bus, do you get furious, angry far beyond what an objective observer might consider an appropriate response to the external provocation? Does this anger derives from your belief that the world is not treating you properly, that you are being dealt a faulty hand? Recent psychological research on happiness indicates that gratitude is an effective antidote to depression. This is an emotion that cannot exist in the context of Neurotic Claims.

Even as the *self-evaluative* consequences of a loss or a rejection can be much greater than the *realistic* consequences, so anger generated on the basis of Claims can add significantly to the impact of everyday hassles. In an interview in *Psychology Today,* stress researcher R. S. Lazarus confirms, "When people get upset over what seem to be trivialities, it's because the trivial symbolizes for them something of tremendous import. When a shoelace breaks, the psychological stress is from the implication that you cannot control your own life, that you're helpless in the face of the most stupid trivialities, or even worse, that such things happen because of your own inadequacies in the first place."

Stress also comes from the sense that you have been thwarted and that you have been denied what you feel entitled to. The key word here is *"entitled."* The important difference between a Claim and a wish or a desire is this feeling of entitlement. While a person may want everything to go smoothly and may feel disappointed when it does not, the individual who has a Claim will *demand* that things go his way and feel furious when they do not. The following list of Claims gives some sense of this *entitlement.* Notice how each Claim takes no notice of other people's rights, feelings, and limitations:

- I am entitled to first-class treatment no matter how I act.
- I don't have to make any major changes to lose weight.
- I have the right to expect that you will call me back immediately.
- I shouldn't have to bother with sexual precautions.
- I should get a raise or promotion without extra effort on my part.
- I should have the benefits of a relationship with no restrictions.
- My children should do as I say.
- My spouse should have the same priorities as I do.
- My spouse should know what I want without my asking.
- I am entitled to your time and money.
- I should never have to wait.
- Because I have suffered, things should go my way.
- Because I have suffered, I should be immune.
- Because I am a man, I shouldn't wash dishes.
- Because I am a woman, I shouldn't have to drive.
- I shouldn't have to work to change myself.
- Because I am your parent, I can order you around.
- If I need something from you, you must comply.
- Other cars should get out of my way.
- You should do what I want you to do.
- You should solve my problems.
- My spouse should pay attention exclusively to me.
- Everything should operate perfectly.
- I should be above criticism.
- The weather should suit my preferences.

- My relatives should give me financial support.
- I shouldn't have to assert myself to get what I want.
- If I have a need, I'm entitled to the best.
- Other people should do things the way I want them done.
- I should be treated as someone who is special.
- You shouldn't hold me responsible for my bad moods.
- Whether or not I can afford it, I should have what I want.
- You should ignore anything that I do when I'm drinking.
- I shouldn't have to work at a job that doesn't fulfill me.
- I shouldn't have to pay interest on this bill.

The pervasiveness of Claims in society today is such that experts have begun to speak of a "psychology of entitlement." In a U. S. *News and World Report* article, "The New Breed of Workers," Jerome Rosow, president of the Work in America Institute, was quoted as saying, "The new generation of workers and their children were conditioned by a boom economy. They have perceived these advantages as normal. Now these expectations have become entitlements." Moreover, according to the U.S. *News* article, "Never in history have American workers been so well paid, so privileged and yet so discontent in their jobs as they are today."

This psychology of entitlement occurred with Bill, a college freshman, who was on the verge of failing biology, his one required college course in natural science. Bill was failing because he wasn't studying. His refusal to study rested on his Claims.

"I can't stand the teacher." was Bill's first explanation of his approaching failure. "He talks to us like we're idiots and requires too much work each night. Then he checks, if you can believe it, to see if we have actually done our homework. That's why I'm failing. I don't like to be regimented. I'm in college. I should be treated like an adult. It's none of his business what I do every night. He shouldn't act like such a grade school teacher."

All of Bill's energy is directed at what he thinks *should* be. He has angered and frustrated himself and is determined not to give in to what he views as an unfair, outmoded method of teaching. Bill claims that he is entitled to have an interesting instructor, one who teaches the way he believes he should be taught. However, Bill, not the teacher, will suffer the *consequences* of this expectation.

When I asked Bill if he wanted to alter his internal Claims, he agreed that he would at least consider it, since he needed to make a passing grade in his course. The reversal in Bill's self-talk progressed in the following manner:

STEP 1: "What am I telling myself?"

"When I sit down to do one of Professor Brown's assignments, I immediately get ticked off. I say to myself, 'This is ridiculous. This assignment is not going to teach me anything. Brown is just an eccentric, rigid, mediocre teacher. Why do I have to put up with this trivia?' This is usually where I shut my book and turn on the radio or grumble to my roommate."

STEP 2: "Is what I'm telling myself helpful?"

"It's not getting my homework done, that's for sure, and I'm not going to get a very good grade in the course unless something changes. No. I suppose it's not useful."

STEP 3: "What are my Drivers, Stoppers, or Confusers?"

"I'm using a lot of labels. If I used an "I" Message, I would say, 'I don't like doing the assignments that Brown is giving me.' I suppose I have a Claim that my schoolwork should always be interesting and that my teachers should be more than mediocre. There's another label. I guess I'm cutting off my nose to spite my face where Brown's concerned."

STEP 4: "What Permission and Self-Affirmation can I give myself?"

"I can say, 'It's okay to have my negative feelings, but I still need to do the work. I'm a good student, and I'm capable of getting a good grade in this class. It's okay for me to do some things that I would rather not do. The world doesn't have to treat me perfectly.'"

STEP 5: "What would my Guide say?"

"Just what I said before. 'It's okay not to like Brown or the assignments, but I still need to do the work. If I stop making myself so angry, I'll have an easier time getting it done.' I can take action by starting the paper that's due next week."

The above dialogue shows that Bill harbored the Claim "I'm entitled to an interesting teacher," as well as a large number of negative labels (rigid, eccentric, mediocre) against his instructor. Labels, such as these, also produce hostility and animosity. They are what we call Anger-Generating Stoppers.

Anger-Generated Stoppers

Stoppers fuel feelings of anger and resentment in two ways. Negatively labeling someone else is the first source of anger. The second is the negative self-labeling of your own impulses to be assertive, a process that inevitably leads to gunnysacking. External labeling or internal labeling, the anger-generating outcome is the same.

The Power of External Labels

You may not realize the power of the external labels that are so much a part of your daily life. Labels provide a compelling, but at the same time, a dangerous simplicity. One label can determine how you will respond to literally millions of people. By labeling, the complexity of human life and the reality of marked individual differences are blotted out. Negative labels generate feelings of resentment, envy, and hate, all major emotional components of prejudice. Directed toward minorities, toward other nationalities, toward women, toward men, toward "anyone over 30", or any other specific groups, labels support the fallacy that all members of a category are alike. Propagandists take full advantage of the power of negative labels to distance and degrade.

When you use negative labels in your day-to-day encounters, the same effect occurs. You distance yourself from and degrade other individuals. Whether these labels are applied in overt communication, or in your thoughts, they encapsulate another person in harsh judgmental terms. A person becomes lazy, inconsiderate, a slob, or a bitch, rather than someone who has simply done something specific that you do not like.

In one of my workshops, the group turned its attention to dealing with this form of anger producing self-talk. Ginger, describing herself as having great resentment toward her roommate Trudy, was the first to volunteer. "Specifically," Ginger related, "Trudy copped out on me when I was expecting her to baby-sit."

"What happened," she continued, "was that I was going out for a special date, and I assumed that Trudy would sit for me. We have an arrangement where I keep her child one weekend night, and she keeps mine another. Since she wanted me to sit for her on Friday, I expected her to sit for me on Saturday. On Saturday morning, however, she told me that she wouldn't be able to stay with my daughter, and I had a lot of trouble trying to find someone else. I've been really angry with her since then, even though it's been a couple of weeks."

After Ginger had described her situation, I asked her if she wanted to change her anger generating self-talk.

"Yes," Ginger agreed, "I'd like to get past these feelings."

She began by asking, "What am I telling myself" "I'm saying that Trudy is insensitive, flaky and irresponsible. I went out of my way the other day to pick her up at work when her car was in the shop, and this is how she pays me back." As an aside, Ginger added, "Now I'm feeling guilty and criticizing myself, 'How can you be so unloving!'"

You may remember from an earlier example how easily blame can shift from oneself to another person. Here the shift is in the reverse direction, from Trudy back to Ginger. Moving from one pole of blame to another is the only alternative possible within the judgmental position.

"Anyway," Ginger continued, "to go on, I want to ask myself if what I'm telling myself is helpful. I don't think it is. I'm walking around the house with my teeth clenched. I don't feel like speaking to Trudy. I'm so angry that I don't even feel like telling her what's bothering me. I just want her to leave."

"What are my Drivers, Stoppers, or Confusers? I know one thing I'm doing. I'm telling myself that because I picked Trudy up at work, she owed it to me to baby-sit on Saturday night. I guess I'm putting a *Be Perfect* Claim on Trudy. I just thought of something else. I'm telling myself that even if I assert myself with her and tell her my feelings, it won't help. I can see that I'm labeling my assertion as *useless*. I also feel that if I say something, I'll make things worse. Who knows? Maybe she would respond."

"Now for the fourth step. I'm supposed to look at Permission and Affirmation and direct it toward Trudy this time. I can say that Trudy doesn't have to be perfect anymore than I do. She didn't know how important Saturday night was to me. She didn't have the full picture. I need to let her know what I expect. That's what I'll do. Next is step five, the action that I plan to take. Maybe the end result will be that Trudy isn't the roommate for me. On the other hand, maybe this is a misunderstanding that we can clear up."

In this example, Ginger demonstrates the anger-producing consequences of the negative external labels (insensitive, flaky, and irresponsible) that she had directed toward Trudy. She also shows how a critical view of another person can combine with any Stoppers already present to block assertive action. This inhibition activates the process of gunnysacking.

The Effect of Internal Labels

Gunnysacking, (the term author George Bach's used for the holding back of negative feelings) leads to the buildup of high levels of tension and hostility. With gunnysacking, we store away each anger-producing incident to be reviewed again and again, each new look fueling the smoldering fires of resentment. When someone annoys you, if you have a gunnysack, the annoying incident will not be considered for itself alone. Instead, it will be examined in conjunction with all the other negative items that you have stored up.

When Candice shows up late for her tennis date, for example, Marie is furious. Candice's lateness brings up for Marie the ten other occasions when she has waited, racket in hand, for Candice to breeze onto the court. Marie has fumed about these prior times to her husband and to her friends. She has not, however, told Candice about her feelings. Afraid to risk appearing *bitchy* or *too demanding*, internal negative labels, Marie has gunnysacked her resentment. So now Candice cannot understand Marie's grim silence, as she gives a perfectly good explanation of her delay.

As you might imagine, gunnysacking is a very common process. Most people are immediately able to identify situations where gunnysacking occurs in their own lives. In one group, a man described himself as having gunnysacks against so many people that he didn't know where to begin in getting rid of them. "By the way," he questioned, "can I get rid of a gunnysack once it is formed?" A woman confessed that she had the world's largest gunnysack, and the world's best memory. She could recall every hurt and resentment that she had thrown into it.

A gunnysack forms when issues are not dealt with at the moment. Because of Stoppers (Negative Self-labels, Catastrophes, and Rigid Requirements), feelings are not expressed spontaneously. Sometimes, they are not asserted at all. Yet unexpressed feelings do not simply go away. You may think that you are leaving them behind as you throw them over your shoulders with an "It's not all that important anyway" disclaimer. Instead of hitting the sidewalk, however, they fall snugly into the ever-present gunnysack. Then, when you are sufficiently angry, tired or fed up not to care any longer, they come pouring out. For men, the gunnysack explosion is typically through anger. For women, the eruption may result in tears of rage. However, the effect is generally the same: embarrassment, guilt, and self-punishment.

To prevent gunnysacking, you need only remove your Stoppers. Then the natural process of self-expression is permitted. Of course, you need not respond so quickly that you ignore the parameters of a situation or fail to consider good timing. However, three days or three months or three years are not required to find a "right time" to assert yourself. Here, the Rigid Requirement, "If the time is right", supports the process of gunnysacking.

When you deal with the internal obstacles that interfere with self-assertion, your feelings and attitudes will change, even when no change occurs externally. Thus, one of my clients described how much more enjoyable his work had become since he had eliminated the Stoppers keeping him from voicing his negative feelings. "I'm under much less stress," he told me, "and I don't have that heavy resentment bearing down on me all the time." Then, upon a moment's reflection, he added, "You know, I just realized. The people I work with haven't really changed at all. It's just that I am no longer taking care of them at my own expense. I now speak up when something bothers me. It's me who has changed."

The removal of a gunnysack reduces anger by allowing you to see each situation as it is, uncontaminated by past feelings of resentment. You do yourself and others a favor when you keep your slate clear.

Letting Go

Unfortunately, there are times when assertion isn't possible. Perhaps the person with whom you need to speak is not available. Perhaps your experience has taught you that the person is unwilling to receive an assertive message. Perhaps the assertion you have made does not affect a change. Do you continue to beat your head against an unfeeling wall? No. There is a second choice. It is within your power to let go of your anger and resentment.

The task of letting go is not an easy one. Propped up as it is on one side by the conviction that the other person is "wrong" or "unfair" and on the other by the judgment that letting go means "failing" or "giving up," the process involves more than a passive decision. It means fully recognizing the cost of chronic, sustained anger. Moreover, it requires actively combating the Stoppers that prevent you from letting go.

Sandra found herself in this position, when for the umpteenth time, her neighbor's dog dug up some of her flowers. As usual, Sandra asserted herself. Once again, however, her straightforward, honest approach did not lead to a positive response on her neighbor's part.

Sandra felt furious that her well-intentioned efforts were ineffective. She did not want to call the police, yet she experienced a mounting rage as her assertion was again and again ignored. Most of Sandra's anger, in fact, rested upon her belief that with a little cooperation things could have been easily resolved. She spent a great deal of energy talking to her husband and her friends about this neighbor. She even caught herself at odd times reviewing what had happened over the past couple of years. A hot flush of hostility came just from thinking about the "numbskull", a label that had settled into Sandra's vocabulary.

Sandra is in a situation where she has been assertive to no avail. She must now "raise her muscle" and take some action other than discussion, or she must let go of her anger-producing thoughts. Since Sandra has decided that she doesn't want to go any further in her action, she agrees that it would be wise to look at changing her internal dialogue. In working on this problem in therapy, Sandra's examined her self-talk:

She first asked, "What am I telling myself?"

Her immediate response was, "I'm saying that my neighbor isn't treating me right. I've been as considerate and as nice as I could be, and she doesn't do anything to help ease the situation. Her dog runs rampant; he's always in my flowers; he barks at night; and…"

I interrupted Sandra. "You could go on and on, couldn't you? Why not consider the cost here? Right now, what are you feeling?"

"You're right," Sandra agreed. "It's amazing to see how easy it is to get right back into those feelings of anger, even when that's not the purpose here. Well, one cost is that I feel very angry, and there's nothing that I can do with that anger. If I were a violent person, I'd wring her neck. But that would get me into trouble, wouldn't it? I know that other people are tired of hearing me bitch about my neighbor's latest idiocy. Something in me, though, doesn't want to let go of it. I feel justified in being angry."

At this point I interjected, "Sandra, who is suffering when you review all these annoyances in your mind? Is it your neighbor, or is it you? You know, during our last few meetings, you've talked more about this neighbor than anyone else. Is she really someone you want to keep carrying around in your head?"

"No, she isn't. Let me see if I can finish this process. I know that I need to consider if there are any Drivers, Stoppers, or Confusers operating. I think that I put Claims on other people. I really do believe that if I behave fairly toward someone else, that person should also behave fairly with me. I get furious when that doesn't happen. It's as if someone is not playing the game the way it's supposed to be played. I guess I'm also into a *Try Hard* Driver. I'm trying hard to make my neighbor see it my way. But, it seems as though I'm beating my head against a wall of stone. I realize that the person suffering right now is me and that I need to let go of my anger and my Claim that my neighbor should treat me fairly. How do I do it?"

"Just continue." I suggested. "Give yourself permission to let your anger go."

I noticed that Sandra leaned back in her chair for the first time. "Okay," she replied. "I give myself permission to stop struggling with this. I've had enough. It's simply costing me, and everyone around me, too much. It's okay to let go of my anger and my struggle. I'm not going to *Try Hard* anymore to make it right."

"Good. What about your Guide?" I asked.

"I don't know," Sandra replied. "I think I've taken all the action relative to my neighbor that I want to take. That's part of letting go, isn't it? I will affirm to my husband and the people I've talked to about her that I'm going to stop concerning myself with the things my neighbor does. And if she ever does anything extreme, I will call the authorities. If not, I'll accept the irritations as part of living."

Before she let go completely, Sandra had to go through this tape change process several times. She had to repeat more than once the reminder "Unfortunately, people don't always treat others fairly. But I don't have to carry the person I dislike most around in my thoughts. Perhaps I learned something from this experience, perhaps not. But I can now let go of my anger."

Anger-Generating Confusers

A final source of self-generated anger derives from Confusers. Each Confuser (Arbitrary Inferences, Misattribution, Cognitive Deficiency, Overgeneralization, Magnification/Discounting, Vague Language, and Either/Or Thinking) has the potential to trigger feelings of anger and resentment. The story about the traveler at the beginning of this chapter is based on Arbitrary Inferences. He formed an arbitrary, negative conclusion, decided it was true, and acted upon it. His inference most likely came from a basic belief such as "you can't trust anyone", "people are undependable", or "everyone's out for number one".

The tendency of the Judge to perceive what's lacking rather than what's present distorts your evaluations of other people. Thus, Keith walks into the house and notices what his wife Betsy hasn't done. The kids' toys are scattered around the room. The beds are unmade. Immediately, he is annoyed. For one thing, Keith has a Claim that if he works outside the home, Betsy should do all the housework. The original decision that Betsy would not pursue her career and take care of the kids has been gradually amended by Keith to include the clause, "full-time housekeeper" as well. Moreover, Keith ignores what Betsy *has* done all day: baking cookies with the kids, paying the bills, and cooking dinner.

A number of Confusers are operating in Keith's self-talk. First is his Claim: "This is too much! Don't I have the right to expect a clean house when I come home from a hard day's work?" Next come *Arbitrary Inference* and *Cognitive Deficiency*: "I guess Betsy feels that she can just laze around all day." This is followed with *Overgeneralization* and *Vague Language*: "Other men don't face this." Finally, it ends with *Magnification*: "This house is a mess."

Unless Keith is willing to examine what he is telling himself, his Confusers will continue to provoke his anger and impair his relationship with Betsy. If his sullenness triggers the same process in Betsy, an increasing distance will develop and ultimately a complete communications breakdown.

A Final Word

The intent of this chapter has *not* been to convey the idea that a person should never feel angry. Your internal signals of anger are very important. Just as a warning pain tells you to remove your hand from a hot surface, anger can give you the emotional momentum to make necessary external changes.

However, it is important that your acceptance of your anger, as well as your assertive expression of it, is tempered by the recognition that anger can be internally generated, through Claims, Confusers, and Stoppers. If other people are frequently viewed as "jerks,"; if negative characteristics suddenly spring up in other people overnight ("I never realized how inconsiderate, obnoxious, and insensitive So-and-So really is"); if you suffer from the negative effects of your anger (tension, interpersonal difficulties, psychosomatic problems), your self-talk may be dosing you with more anger than is necessary. This anger is not an Intrinsic Self protective response. By examining your own anger generating self-talk, you can free yourself from this chronic judgmental condition and from the extra stress of living with chronic resentment.

CHAPTER 11

The Development of Negative Self Talk

I was haunted for many years by the question, "Why?" Have you wondered about your own self-dialogue? Why do you castigate yourself? Why do you limit yourself with prohibitions that seem to have no reason? Why do you talk to yourself, and sometimes others, in destructive ways? Isn't the human organism oriented toward growth? Doesn't negative self-talk counter human evolution, since it leads to physical disease and psychological unhappiness? Is it possible that this strange and counter-productive way of operating in the world is in some way a necessary adaptation? Were your current self-hindering behaviors once necessary to your very survival? Could the same self-talk that now generates depression, and even suicide, have originated in decisions that were literally life saving at an earlier time?

But how could the demands of survival lead you to numb yourself, to lock your feelings away, to forget a part of your experience? The answer to this riddle lies in the fact that the Intrinsic Self operates in the service of the organism *as a whole*. Just as an animal caught in a steel-jawed trap will gnaw its paw off in order to escape, so the Intrinsic Self will stifle or block itself in an attempt to adapt to a situation where normality is dangerous.

As Alice Miller emphasized in her books *For Your Own Good* and *Thou Shalt Not Be Aware,* it is not merely the trauma of abuse with which a child must deal, but also the lack of permission to grieve, process, or express the emotion generated by the trauma. "If you don't stop crying, I'll give you something to cry about," affirms this in brutal terms. When the environment is abusive, a child will construct a psychological template to minimize the amount of abuse she must face. Once constructed, this painfully drawn map continues to operate *on its own* even when the environment changes. Though once necessary, this map burdens the child with obstructions (Stoppers), commands (Drivers) and other miscellaneous self talk (Confusers) that make no sense in terms of present-day realities. Because we all operate to some extent from such maps, we all need help in differentiating or discriminating past from present.

A joke illuminates this point. A client enters psychotherapy with a strange behavior. The client constantly snaps his fingers. The therapist, being non-directive, ignores this behavior for some time, until finally her curiosity gets the best of her, and she asks, "Why do you keep snapping your fingers like that?" The client replies, "Oh, I thought you knew. It's to keep the lions and tigers away." The therapist, incredulous, responds, "But there are no lions and tigers around here." The client, with infinite patience, agrees, "Well, it works quite well, thank you."

Do you, like this client, continue to act in ways that make no sense when taken in the current context? Do you operate by defensive maneuvers, your own "finger snapping", to avoid the reappearance of your demons?

The Judge as Protector

Now, in a more specific frame, let's examine how statements, such as "I'm not good enough", "Something's wrong with me", "I can't depend on anyone else", "No one could love me", or "I'm stupid" have served to protect one from the pain of past childhood traumas. Consideration of the following five hypotheses will allow you to make sense of these punitive self-messages:

(1) Originally, the Judge develops to protect a child from the adverse elements in his environment, most particularly from a parent, frequently from a teacher, a sibling, or an abusive member of his peer group. This protection takes the form of negative self-talk.

(2) The Judge is no more severe or brutal than the environment necessitates.

(3) Examining the Judge leads to the discovery of forgotten or hidden elements in an individual's childhood.

(4) The Judge allows an individual to hold her parents and other caretakers in the best possible light, thereby maintaining hope.

(5) An individual holds to his Judge because its function has been vitally necessary to his survival.

I first formulated these hypotheses while working with a client diagnosed with Dissociative Identity Disorder (commonly referred to as multiple personality). Here, an extreme form of splitting or separating of one self from another occurs. Frequently, one self is pure Judge, seemingly brutal and vindictive toward the other selves. This self holds or "contains" the painful memories that protect the other selves. In my work with a client whom I'll call Jane, this persecutory self was clearly present. Whenever Jane felt or attempted to express genuine feelings, she would become extremely anxious, and switch into a second persecutory self, Judy. Judy would do whatever she could to stop these soft or vulnerable feelings, hitting her head with her fists or biting her arms. When I attempted to restrain Judy, her anxiety would increase into panic. After a point, this anxiety would peak, and Jane would again return.

In the process of working with Jane's persecutory self, Judy, I discovered the circumstances in which she became necessary for Jane's survival. Jane's mother would explode and beat Jane mercilessly whenever Jane expressed feelings or needs. However, when Jane/Judy would hit herself, her mother would stop her own vastly more threatening abuse. Moreover, when Judy could stop Jane from expressing or even experiencing these normal feelings, there was much less chance of her mother's going "crazy" and brutalizing her. By her abuse, Judy, the developing Judge, was actually attempting to protect Jane, the real child. In all probability, by doing so she saved Jane's life.

After seeing this process operate so dramatically, it became clear to me that no matter how bizarre certain behaviors appear to be in the present, these behaviors had a function in the past and that this function was survival. My respect for this inner protective mechanism increased as I worked with Jane and her second personality, Judy.

If you examine your own Judge from this perspective, it will give you direct evidence about your early environment. Physical punishment, ridicule, withdrawal of love, psychological or physical abandonment, or the threat of abandonment all have great influence upon a child. Rather than risk losing a parent's love, a child will discard valuable parts of himself. Because the Judge develops so early, you may have no memory of what led to its development. Moreover, you will naturally resist the painful memories or feelings experienced from being reared by imperfect parents, even those who were doing their best. But beyond the mere forgetting of childhood memories, two other factors help to blur the connection between the Judge and one's early environment. One of these is the adaptability of the child; the other is the ability of a child to live in fantasy and denial.

Adaptability is demonstrated by what has been called the "good child syndrome." Some children learn very quickly the rules of the family. They are often highly sensitive individuals who require very little punishment to conform. Other children, particularly those with Attention Deficit and Hyperactive Disorder, have a more difficult time constructing the inner brakes necessary for compliance and thus receive a much higher amount of negative repercussions. The very adaptable child, however, may be so well behaved that he receives very little punishment or reproach. As adults, these individuals rarely remember any reasons for their severe internal Judges.

The second impediment against remembering one's childhood is denial. Parents are viewed in a falsely idealized manner. Horrifying childhood experiences are transformed into the belief, "I had a happy childhood." This common delusion exists because the negativity, which was part of the child's early upbringing, is absorbed by the Judge and directed against the Real Self. The child decides that "Something's wrong with me" and "I'm not good enough", rather than face the truth of the neglect or abuse in his family of origin. Such decisions allow some sense to be made of the toxic environment without having all hope dashed. As the child's reasoning goes, "If the fault is mine, then maybe I can change. If I am just better, smarter, nicer, or if I stop causing a bother, having needs, or being different, then things will change. The environment isn't awful. It's me." Thus, the Judge transforms a bad situation into one where there is hope. With hope, the child continues to live, albeit with an increasingly heavy weight of internal Drivers, Stoppers, and Confusers.

In making a simple image of all of this, I sometimes say to my clients, "To keep your Mom and Dad on a pedestal, you had to lie on the floor." In other words, to idealize your parents, you have chosen to denigrate yourself. Accepting your own parents as human beings, often with very real and profound practical and emotional limitations, is very difficult. Much grief is required to let go of the illusion of their having been or their ever becoming the parents that you wanted, needed, or even deserved. But this acceptance is part of the work necessary in dismantling the Judge, and consequently, getting yourself up off the floor.

The upside-down framework just described creates an interesting paradoxical experience, where an individual will fight against receiving positive feedback. Frequently, a client refuses to believe anything positive about herself. My comments are discounted, "Oh, you have to say that; you're my therapist," implying that I would lie in order to try to help her. Clients cling to their negative attitudes, because to accept a new view is to risk the return of the lions and tigers. As one client shared, "I'd be totally devastated if I believed you liked me and then found out I was a fool and that you didn't. I'd rather not take that risk." For someone who was punished for any good feelings ("Don't get a big head," "Who do you think you are?" "You're getting too big for your britches"), or given a slap across the face whenever a spontaneous or genuine feeling was expressed, letting go of the negative squelchers can be experienced as a life-or-death proposition.

Another story illustrates this dilemma. A man fell off a ship and was struggling to stay afloat. The people on deck threw him a life preserver, but each time he attempted to grab for it, he went under again. It became clear that he was clinging to a sack of rocks that were pulling him down. Someone on board ship cried out, "Hey man, drop those rocks." The drowning sailor replied, "But they're *my* rocks." Can you wholeheartedly and honestly deny having felt, "But they're my beliefs. I'm too frightened to let them go"?

Again questions emerge: "Why do you need to protect yourself from seeing reality as it is? Why is it preferable to turn against yourself instead of recognizing the truth? Why do you create illusions that turn out to be the rocks that hold you down?" To understand these seeming paradoxes, one must realize that the attachments children form with parents, even bad parents, are necessary for their survival. There exists without doubt an instinctual basis for this attachment. Take birds, which attach or "imprint" to the first moving object they see upon hatching. Dr. Kenneth Melvin found that he could imprint baby quail to a sparrow hawk, the quail's natural enemy in the wild. The baby quails followed the hawk, even when the hawk made threatening and aggressive movements toward them. Nature, in this case, seemed convinced that attachment serves a higher purpose than avoidance. The instinct to follow was greater than the instinct to flee. So the Judge operates to allow a child to hold the parent in the best possible light, enabling the child to maintain her attachment to the parent, even when the parent is abusive or unavailable.

Of course the absolute reality for most children is that they cannot leave their family situations, even if they want to. Many of my clients at one time or another attempted to run away from home. Many others fantasized that their real parents would soon come to find them and take them away from the harmful or non-nurturing environments in which they currently lived. But in the end, all had to adjust to their particular families, whatever their dysfunctions. If such choices were available to children, perhaps the decision to turn against the Intrinsic Self would not occur. Negative self-labels and destructive attitudes could be handed back, "Thanks, but no thanks."

Handing the Labels Back

As an adult, you can now make this choice. You can hand back the negative labels and judgments to the people and to the environment in which they belong. You can get up off the floor, as you take other people off their undeserved pedestals. This is what Rose was able to do. Rose considered herself a "misfit." When someone carries a label like this, it is often quite easy to discover where it came from simply by asking, "How does that label fit you as a little kid?" Or, as I asked Rose, "How old do you feel right now?"

ROSE: "I feel like I'm seven."

ME: "What's happening to you at seven years old?"

ROSE: "I'm in school, and I'm seeing all my friends, and they have really nice parents and nice homes, and they fit in, and I don't."

ME: "How don't you fit in?"

ROSE: "Well, I don't fit in with my father. I can never please him."

ME: "Do you think that any little girl would fit in with your father?" *(Rose's father happened to be an extremely violent and self-centered man.)*

ROSE: "Probably not."

ME: "Who's the real misfit? Is it you as a little girl, or is it your father?"

As my questions began to have an impact, Rose's face lit up, and she spontaneously asserted to her father, "Hey, I'm not a misfit! Nobody could fit in with you!"

After all those years, the label "misfit" was put back to where it belonged. Rose no longer had to protect her father by believing she was bad. In handing the label back, Rose began to rid herself of a critical basic belief. She no longer needed to walk into a room carrying with her the label "misfit", or self-talk such as "You're not going to fit in", "Nobody's going to like you", or "You might as well not have come here."

Because Rose, as an adult, no longer needs her father to be okay at any cost, she can leave this negative attribute with her father where it really belongs.

Thanking Your Judge

Given that (1) the Judge protects the Child, (2) the Judge is no more brutal than the environment necessitates, (3) the Judge maintains hope of change, and (4) the Judge helps to prevent early childhood pain, it is important that you give your Judge a proper acknowledgment. As a prelude to letting go of your Judge, an expression of appreciation is often appropriate. I have found that the Judge is more willing to retire when this acknowledgment is given.

A clear example of this occurred recently. I was using a two-chair technique with one of my clients, Diane. We were examining the role her Judge played in keeping her under rigid control. (In the two-chair technique, a person alternates between two chairs, talking respectively as her Judge and as her Intrinsic Self.) I asked Diane to sit in one chair and to assume the role of her inner controller, or Judge. But instead of confronting her Judge as an enemy, I chose to acknowledged the value that the Judge had provided. I ventured, "I bet you really had to keep Diane under control as a little girl, so that she would be safe."

Diane's eyes welled up with tears as she replied, "Yes, she would get hit if I didn't."

I then asked Diane's Judge, "Is that what happened when she talked back?"

Diane replied, "There was just one right way to do things."

I said, "Oh, in your family, there must not have been much room to be spontaneous or different."

As we talked further, I acknowledged the importance of Diane's original decision to control herself. To her Judge/Controller, I empathized, "I know how important you were to Diane. You protected her very well in her family."

Diane, still crying, asked if she could thank her Judge. "I want to thank you for keeping me quiet, because you knew I would be hurt. Thank you." She sobbed quietly for a moment and then added, "But I want you to know that now I'm big, and I won't let anyone hit or yell at me ever again, so you can stop controlling me. I no longer need you to protect me, but thank you for being there a long time ago."

Diane cried softly for a few more minutes and then looked up as if to say, "Okay, I'm ready to move on."

Discriminating Past from Present

We all are born with the capacity to generalize. If I touch a hot stove, I'm more careful the next time I approach any stove, not just the one that burned me. This capacity to generalize, particularly around pain, is a survival adaptation. Discrimination learning, in contrast, is about noticing difference. The cat, which scratched me last year, is different from the cat approaching me now. I don't automatically need to be afraid.

The conditioning that occurs in childhood leads to great generalization, particularly when pain is involved. Without knowing it, you may frequently over-generalize, treating *now* as if it were *then*. This over-generalized way of behaving operates unconsciously, making it even more pernicious. In order to discriminate past from present, an active reevaluation process needs to occur.

This was true for Jim, a two-hundred-pound athlete, who felt, "I'm always backed into a corner"

While working with Jim, I suggested, "Would you be willing to walk into the middle of the room and see why it's not safe there for you?"

I continued, "Will you imagine your mother approaching and see if she interferes with your motion?"

Jim imagined his mother and said, "Oh. I've got to face the same direction that she does."

Jim's early decision to protect his mother meant that he would do things just like she wanted. Once Jim asserted to his mother that he was resigning that job, he took back his ability to look around the room.

Next, I asked Jim to imagine his father getting up. Jim responded, "No, with him here, I've got to stand in the corner, because I don't trust him. He might hurt me."

This was absolutely true when Jim was a little boy. He had an abusive father.

At this point I asked Jim, "How tall were you as a little boy, when you were so frightened of your dad?"

He guessed, "Three feet."

I asked him, "How tall are you now?"

"Six feet."

I followed with the question, "Can your father hurt you now?"

Jim laughed and said, "He can't hurt me now!" and the spell was broken.

By understanding the early development of negative self-talk, its purpose in survival, and the ubiquitous failure to differentiate *now* from *then,* you now have a solid intellectual base for understanding your negative self-talk. This, in turn, will help you drop the rocks of your negative beliefs, and encourage you to stop your automatic finger snapping. The final chapter, "Listening to Your Self," will give you the tools to discover that the lions and tigers are long gone, and the need for struggle and self-limitation no longer exists.

CHAPTER 12

Listening to Yourself

To thine own self be true and it must follow, as the night the day, thou canst not then be false to any man." In this famous passage from *Hamlet*, Shakespeare challenges you to listen to yourself.

"How *do* I listen to myself?" Amber asked after confessing that she had spent the drive to her appointment thinking about a "stupid" concern.

I gently suggested that Amber share this concern. "Maybe the thoughts and feelings, which occupy your radar screen right now, aren't so stupid. Maybe they have some important information for you, if you are willing to listen."

Amber thought for a moment, nodded and then cautiously replied, "It's just that I have a friend whom I haven't heard from in awhile, and I miss her."

We spent the rest of the session talking about this friend and the various Stoppers that were in the way of Amber's writing or calling her. The session was rich and productive, her concern linked to many central issues. Yet Amber's Judge had easily dismissed this entire topic as "stupid". Had I not challenged this negative label, Amber would have delayed dealing with this important piece of information.

Amber's question, "How do I listen to myself?" is valid for everyone. Which part of yourself do you listen to anyway? Do you listen to your automatic voice (the Judge), which negates and discounts? Or, do you treat your subtler, less self-righteous, voice with attention and respect?

Thankfully, intrinsic feelings and needs continue to resurface, even when discounted or ridiculed. The Intrinsic Self struggles mightily to push through the asphalt of the Judge. In short, you will have many opportunities to learn to listen to yourself.

From this perspective, I reassured Amber, "What you need to hear will keep coming into your consciousness, much as you want to dismiss it. But wouldn't it feel better for you to accept this need's polite knock before it assaults you with a two-by-four depression?"

Listening to yourself remains the best way to discover your Intrinsic Self. This Self speaks when you are willing to listen. Messages delivered through feelings, images, dreams, and even physical symptoms can break through the most rigid, judgmental structures. Sifting this gold from the sand of your everyday inner chatter is now your final task."

Feelings

Your feelings provide you with vital information about your Intrinsic Self. Encountering your intrinsic feelings is like discovering a vein of gold within your being, a deep current of emotion that is lasting and profound. Sometimes, tears accompany these feelings. In *The Wounded Woman*, these tears are explained as the keys that unlock the doors to hidden palaces within.

Fritz Perls, the founder of Gestalt Therapy, describes these deep feelings as comprising the explosive voice of the self, hidden under layers of phoniness, role-playing and deadness. Explosions into grief, anger, and joy are frequently elicited in therapy or whenever another person listens with compassion. You can connect with this deep inner current within yourself through journal writing or through successive repetitions of the Five Step Method. Unpeeling the onion, as some have called it, leads to the emergence of deeper and deeper layers, each closer to your true self. Francine Shapiro, the developer of the therapy technique called EMDR, has altered this image of the onion to that of an artichoke. After peeling back enough layers, you arrive at your heart.

Contrast the true messages from the Intrinsic Self to the noise or static generated by the Judge. The Judge can and does provide a steady stream of negative feeling loops. Depression loops contain self-talk like, "You'll never accomplish anything," "You're just a failure," "You'll never get what you want," or "No one cares about you." Anger loops put the blame on others, but not in a manner that will lead to successful assertion, negotiation, or change. Self-talk themes like "He never cares about me", "She's just out for herself", or "Life isn't fair", generate chronic anger. Fear loops, such as "Be careful", "You may say the wrong thing", or "No one will like you", will keep you out of the game entirely.

The emotions generated by the Judge lead to impulsive acting out or chronic, all-pervasive feeling-attitudes. Instead of assertion motivated by the energy of anger, you get aggression or seething hostility, dry and brittle. Instead of the sadness that activates healing grief, you feel chronic depression and an inability to cry. Your fear does not lead to self-protection, but to chronic worry about things over which you have little or no control. The

Judge generates emotions, which damage your happiness, and destroy your relationships with others.

In contrast, the emotions of the Intrinsic Self lead to considered action. These feelings or intuitions give you information about an activity, a person or a situation that is simply not available through mere thought. Whether it is an apartment to rent, a house to buy, a dress to wear, a person to go out with, how you actually feel is paramount. Listen to that queasy feeling inside your stomach! Even if you tell yourself there is no good reason not to accept a date, or sign a lease, if you are not experiencing a sense of confidence, comfort or excitement, look again. There is rarely, if ever, a need to push or prod when one is connected to the inner well of energy and aliveness of the Intrinsic Self.

To discriminate between the emotions generated by the Judge and the emotions arising from your Intrinsic Self, examine your self-talk. Words, like "should," "ought," and "have to", are favored by the Judge. In contrast, "I want", "I love doing this", or "I get to" usually derive from your Real Self. Beware of the impulsive voice of the Sit Down Strike saying, "To hell with it", "Who gives a damn", or "I might as well do it". This voice is also operating against the interest of your Intrinsic Self. Its rebellious line will not generate true self-determination.

Dreams

A good friend of mine found herself in a job that did not suit her, leaving her depressed during the day and tearful at night. She dreamed of a great killer whale caught in a tiny pond without enough room to move, just as she herself was stagnating. One of my clients, a medical doctor, dreamed that she was operating on a patient without anesthesia. As she cut into the patient's flesh, the patient raised up and screamed at her, "You're hurting me!" a shocking and disturbing message that led her to examine how she was treating herself. Another client had a dream in which she was told to treat a large extended family of people. The only problem was that everyone was talking at once, and she couldn't get a word in edgewise. She walked outside to get a cup of coffee and when she returned, her boss criticized her for leaving the scene. In her non-dream life, her Scare Talk, Blame Talk, and Should Talk constantly prevented her from moving in any clear direction. She experienced many voices, but no one functioned to mediate their different agendas. As her dream clarified, she needed a strong inner therapist to take charge.

You have many voices inside yourself. This inner family may interact to create a toxic environment, in much the same way that real families can be toxic to its members. A tyrant-ruled family is replicated on the inside when one part of the self, usually the Judge, rules with a punishing barrage of negative self-talk while the other members hide in fear or shame or wage a hidden guerrilla war against the inner controller.

Liz Walker agreed to share a dream, which she beautifully writes about in the passage that follows. Liz shows us how dreams can convey, in a creative story, many important and unclaimed parts of ourselves. Identifying with these diverse characters and voices gives you great insight into the present state of your actual situation and helps you to clarify the direction in which you need to move. Following the method of Fritz Perls, Liz tells her dream in the present tense.

The air is warm, the ground churned to dust two and three inches deep by military vehicles. I am attached to a South American army division along with several other United States civilians, and it is moving out. Soldiers are packing, loading trucks, and leaving the area.

Word comes that the enemy is closing in, so activities speed up. Men are running about, shouting. I call out directions to my civilian comrades, but we have not been organized properly. There is no agreed plan so my efforts are ineffectual.

Across the wide brown river, I see the enemy army, limbs swinging in proud unison, eight and twelve abreast, moving along the other bank, southward, to where I know a bridge is located. Each is dressed exactly like the hundreds of others: drab green tunic, black shirt, and long straight black native-born hair. It is an army made up entirely of women!

My pulse races, breath stuck in my throat. I yell to a colleague but he pays no attention to me. I am on my own, searching frantically for a way out or a place to hide, clambering over containers on the last outbound truck, seeking a niche, a place to wedge my body, and failing to find one, drop to the ground.

Enemy voices close in. There is no foliage to hide me. I dive in the dirt, thinking to still my heart and breathe, to act like a casualty of war, already dead, not worthy of their attention.

Soldiers enter the clearing. I feel their presence not more than six feet away. I hear a slight metallic sound; I sense the M16 pointing at my back. Dust grits between tongue and teeth as I melt into its warmth, my body a frozen cage of fear in the hot sun.

I woke from the dream in a panic, hit first by the imminence of death, then by the dream's dire prediction. Was this to be the sum of my life: a hopeless victim?

"Tell me about yourself as the guerrilla soldier," Pam replied.

"But I'm not the soldier. That's the whole point! I'm the goddamned victim on the ground. The soldier's going to kill me."

I had related the dream to Pam almost without breath, running words together in a way that had become familiar to us both over our relationship as patient and psychotherapist. I first sought her help after my mother died, when I couldn't stop crying and moping about. We met once a week, dissecting every feeling I could muster about the woman who had dominated my life, for whose affection I had yearned and worked, and whom I never pleased nor ever really knew.

As my feelings got rearranged, my growing strength caused other dislocations that called for Pam's guidance and support: the most important one a long, drawn-out, very messy divorce. Pam had seen me through death and taxes, loves and jobs, and several significant personal losses. Through it all she got to know, indeed helped to shape, the inside configuration of my being, and could thus comprehend very readily my words and their meanings in a given situation. In short, we were on the same wavelength.

"You're all the parts of your dream," Pam said. "Now, tell me about yourself as the soldier."

It was quiet in the bright little office as I stilled my breathing. My eyes ran a tiny figure-8 round and round a dirty spot in the carpet. I squeezed them shut as I thought of myself in the soldier's role. "She is…I am…committed to a cause," I said. "I am very disciplined. And focused. Very clear about the job I have to do. I am defender and protector of my beautiful country. And I'm righteously angry with its invaders. I am dedicated and supremely capable of carrying out my responsibilities and winning our freedom."

"Good. Now, tell me about yourself as the country."

"I've been abused by outsiders for centuries." I was really in it now. "My resources depleted by them for their gain—my own people denigrated, mistreated, denied their rightful stature and position. But I still have valuable natural resources. It is now time for my people to take charge, harness these resources, and use them for our common good…. My God."

There was silence in the room.

"That is a powerful dream," Pam said.

"God. I'm not just the victim?"

"The victim is your old self. The way you used to be. The way you once had to be to get along. Now you have other choices."

"I'm the soldier. The country. The whole goddamned army of women soldiers."

"Your dream is telling you this."

Silence.

"If so I can become a guerrilla soldier. Dedicated. Focused. Disciplined. That's my way to go."

"Sounds good."

"I need to preserve my resources…energy, talent, money, time. Stop frittering myself away trying to please people. Trying to get approval."

"Yes."

"Christ, it's hard."

"I know it is. But you can do it."

"Yes. If I think like a soldier, it becomes clear. Thank you. Thank you so much." My eyes spilled rivers.

"It's your dream. And your interpretation! There is no need to thank me."

"Yes. It's my dream. It's my guerrilla warrior. But you gave me the way to understand it. Thank you."

In the following weeks and months, Liz returned to her dream. By anchoring herself as the warrior instead of the victim, Liz was able to confront and master many difficult situations in new and powerful ways. I particularly enjoy dreams like the one Liz wrote for herself. In dreams like these, hidden powers and capabilities manifest themselves in frightening and unlikely characters.

Images

It is possible that Images have saved my life. By listening to their messages, I have changed direction. These Images have appeared when it became necessary for my Intrinsic Self to send me crucial warnings. Often my Judge had failed so miserably to solve a problem that, in a state of exhaustion, it quit the center stage for a moment and allowed another part of me to emerge.

One such Image involved a client that I was attempting to rescue. Her suicidal behavior was both provocative and serious, and I found myself emotionally hooked into *Trying Hard* to save her. I felt terribly inadequate. It seemed that whatever I attempted backfired or was "not good enough." This is, of course, typical Rescuer self-talk. I generally avoid getting caught in the Rescue dilemma. However, her genuine anguish, accompanied by both suicidal threats and attempts, was strong enough to trigger my old reactions. Moreover, I was still hanging tight to certain illusions about myself and had not fully accepted my own human limitations. I was unwilling to see that the ultimate responsibility for her life was her own. Furthermore, I did not wish to admit that I had very little actual control over what she did.

Pondering this dilemma one day, an image appeared in my consciousness. I was swimming out into the ocean, drifting farther and farther from the shore, in an attempt to "save" my client, who was headed at an even faster pace into the open sea. Witnessing myself in this "motion picture", I had the immediate sense that if I swam any farther, I would not be able to make my own way back to safety. I would drown. This image impacted me greatly since I had almost drowned in the ocean several years previously and saved myself only by clear, authoritative positive self-talk.

This image made it very clear that I was in over my head. As the old cliché goes, "A picture is worth a thousand words." I acknowledged my dilemma and the seriousness and fragility of my own position. I realized that my attempts at Rescue might even have been reinforcing her suicidal behavior. Finally, I let go.

The spontaneous occurrence of imagery is very powerful. You can supplement this automatic process by asking yourself for information and by being receptive to the answers when they come, be they in the form of pictures, words, or dreams.

The idea of using imagery to heal was originated by the three cancer specialists, Dr. Carl Simonton, Stephanie Mathews-Simonton, and James Creighton in their book *Getting Well Again.* These investigators found that people could contribute to their own healing by the thoughts and images they themselves generated. Imagining that great white sharks were eating and destroying cancer cells was one of the exercises found to be useful with cancer patients considered to have severely progressed diseases.

In his book *Healing Yourself,* Dr. Martin Rossman describes the use of imagery to get in touch with an Inner Healer (similar to our Guide). This Healer, visualized in pictorial form, sometimes as a wise person and sometimes as an animal, can speak to us from the wisdom of the Intrinsic Self. You have the capacity to create this inner resource. If you doubt this, just remember the creativity you express in the dreams you compose each and every night.

A parable that I would like to leave with you is found in the *Teaching of Buddha.* A man is walking alongside a river whose ground is difficult to traverse because it is covered with rocks, brush, and trees. He notices that the opposite riverbank appears much gentler, a beach of sand, with no heavy brush impeding the way. Therefore, he decides to build a raft and cross to the other side. Indeed, upon crossing the river, he finds this bank to be flat and without the obstacles he had left behind. Feeling relieved, he picks up the heavy wooden raft, which he made to cross the river, hoists it over his back, and proceeds with difficulty on his journey. The question is asked, "Is this a wise man?"

Symptoms

Physical symptoms give you the message that you need to listen to your feelings, images, and dreams. The Judgmental Self has been unwilling to yield the conductor's baton and, in the famous line from *The Godfather*, the Intrinsic Self has been forced to give you a message you cannot refuse to hear.

A client of mine (whom I'll call Jason) was given such a message, when he collapsed with back pain. Jason found himself literally flat on his back, unable to meet what had become a murderous schedule of obligations. Since these were all "good things" that he wanted to do and felt he should do, Jason had not even considered his personal, physical, and psychological limitations. He felt pride in the level of his work output and, conversely, shame around the idea that he needed to do less.

At first, Jason was furious at his back. "It's not supposed to do that," he complained. Jason thought of his body as a machine and was appalled when it had any physical needs or requirements. People with such attitudes are usually mimicking the toxic messages from their early life, when parents, in a hurry and under stress, got mad at them for taking too long in the bathroom or for getting sick.

Jason's back did not get well just because his Judge commanded it. As a result, for the first time in his life, Jason had to sit still. Unable to run from himself through work and physical activity, he had to become acquainted with his inner self. Jason began to relax and to experience pleasurable feelings that he had never known. Suddenly, he had permission to read, to meditate, to think and plan, all activities that had been obliterated by his compulsive "to do" lists. As he recovered, he began to identify the small signals of overstress that had preceded his back-related emergency. By setting limits with others, he continued to give himself time and space. Unexpectedly, by being more selective and making room for his creativity, Jason became even more successful. Regardless of notions to the contrary, the rules and demands of the Judgmental position often prevent high achievement. They almost certainly keep us from achieving happiness.

A poem I once wrote, entitled *Prisons*, contained a refrain that fits here:

> *For prisons are inside you*
> *Not inside of wood or stone*
> *And you and I may ride away*
> *If we slay the rules, alone.*

The rules that are handed down...John Bradshaw has said that what you don't hand back to your parents, you hand down to your children. But in handing back the judgmental rules, you leave your internal prison, and give yourself new Permissions. These too, you can pass on.

The Cost of Not Listening

In his excellent book *Anatomy of an Illness*, Norman Cousins devotes an entire chapter to the topic "Pain is not the Ultimate Enemy." Cousins states, "The most ignored fact of all about pain is that the best way to eliminate it is to eliminate the abuse. Instead, many people reach almost instinctively for the painkillers, such as aspirins, barbiturates, codeines, tranquilizers, sleeping pills, and dozens of other analgesics or desensitizing drugs."

Cousins defends the validity of pain as a signal of abuse, highlighting the work of Dr. Paul Brand with the dread disease of leprosy. Dr. Brand discovered that the principal effect of leprosy is to kill nerve endings. Most of the debilitating characteristics of leprosy (missing fingers and toes, blindness) are not specific manifestations of the disease process itself but instead result from the loss of pain receptors. People with leprosy don't remove their hands from a hot surface, resulting in severe injury. Further, they do not blink their eyes when they begin to get dry, ultimately leading to blindness.

In summarizing the work of Paul Brand, Cousins comments, "He is a doctor who, if he could, would move heaven and earth just to return the gift of pain to people who do not have it, for pain is both the warning system and the protective mechanism that enables an individual to defend the integrity of his body. Its signals may not always be readily intelligible, but at least they are there. And the individual can mobilize his response."

I was so impressed by this account that I shared it with many of my clients. If the term *anger* or *sadness* were to be substituted for the word *pain,* I believe that the message would still hold true. Also, feelings are the means by which the Intrinsic Self tells you that you need to alter your current state. They inform you that the messages of the Imposed Self are too severe or that the external environment is toxic and needs changing. When you ignore these messages and do not permit their awareness, you resemble the person with leprosy. Important receptors have been silenced, and you are vulnerable to assault.

Just as the person with leprosy will often injure himself physically, if you do not listen to and honor feelings of fatigue or sadness or depression, you are prone to injuring yourself. Paula held to a philosophy summed up in her comment, "Well, if I *can* do it, then why not?" The "why not" relates to the cost.

Once you begin to listen to your Intrinsic Self, you may find that your real interests have very little to do with your present occupation. You may discover that your current lifestyle does not permit you to spend time doing what you enjoy most. You may find that your relationship with your friends is based on little more than a mutual rescue operation. You may even discover that your love relationship has little connection to your Intrinsic Self.

Opening up to this kind of discovery, makes you aware of just how costly it is to deny your Intrinsic Self. For some, letting go of their Imposed Self becomes a question of physical or psychological survival. I have worked with several people for whom the choice was either developing a new way of protecting and nurturing themselves or complete collapse. I distinctly remember one of my clients saying, "I had the choice of getting myself an office/retreat or of paying ten times that amount in a hospital." Pushed against the judgmental wall, life-threatening illnesses (cancer, diabetes, coronary heart disease) tell someone to change or die. As Shirley Luthman notes in *Collection 1979*, "Some people's rigid structures are so powerful that only the threat of physical death would shake them."

Taking the Leap

After many years of unhappiness, Linda trusted herself enough to leave a financially secure and socially prestigious marriage. From the very beginning of her divorce, she experienced a newfound sense of comfort and wellbeing. Yet even with this strong inner confirmation of her decision, she continued to doubt her actions on a moment-to-moment basis.

Fortunately, Linda listened to the feedback emerging from her own insides. As she told me, "Something new has happened. The other day I found myself smiling, just because I felt so good. Not smiling at anyone, not smiling for any particular reason, but smiling because I like me, and I like what I'm doing. I'd never done that before—ever!"

Along with feelings of wellbeing, an increase in energy will occur when you follow your own inner signals. Linda also described new ideas about what she wanted to do with her life. It was as if she were dealing a deck of cards in front of us both. "Can you believe how many ideas I had this week?" Linda exclaimed. "And they just came to me. And I've had so much energy. It's almost like I'm floating. There's no longer any gravity." Linda's energy is reflecting not only her new environment but also her new decision to stop punishing and depressing herself.

Following your Intrinsic Self will result in lowered stress. By refusing to drive or push beyond your own natural pace, you will gear the level of stress in your life to your capability level. You can become what cancer experts Carl Simonton and Stephanie Mathews-Simonton call "weller than well."

Accepting Others

As you begin to accept and honor your Intrinsic Self, you also tend to give other people this same degree of understanding and permission. You begin to allow them to learn from their own emotions and to listen to their own internal signals.

Nowhere is this kind of support more important than in dealing with children. You can allow them to walk along the symbolic sidewalk, learning from their own mistakes, or you can force them onto a tightrope of perfectionism, which in the end creates inhibited or rebellious reactions.

Jamie was raised on such a judgmental tightrope. Although she was now an adult and a parent herself, she continues to react to her mother's Judge as she did when she was small. Half in jest, Jamie shared with me a prototype of her conversation with her mother.

MOTHER: "How are you?"
JAMIE: "Fine."
MOTHER: "What's new?"
JAMIE: "Nothing."
MOTHER: "Where are you going?"
JAMIE: "Out."

I remarked to Jamie, "That's one way to keep her Judge out of commission," and she broke into peals of laughter. "I never quite thought of it like that, but you're right. There's a lot going on right now that I would like to share with my mother, but she would start picking things apart, and I'm not yet strong enough to deal with that, so I shut her out. Knowing my reactions to my own mother, I'm very careful not to respond judgmentally to my own kids. I want them to be there, even if I don't think they're doing everything exactly right."

In *A Private Battle,* Cornelius Ryan tells of his relationship with his son Geoff:

"Geoff wasn't always sullen and withdrawn. When he was four or five, there was a constant happiness caught often by my camera, a joy of life and love of people. Did we stamp it out? Did I try too hard to make him a fisherman, a hunter, an athlete? Did Kathryn try too hard to make him a scholar? We wanted only the best for him but on *our* terms; it was always *our* view of what was best. When he tried and failed to manage a task we'd set, we'd put him over the jumps again. Is it any wonder we find him, now just past seventeen, sullen and antagonistic?"

Ryan is talking of the demands that parents place on the developing child, because they feel responsible to "Make Sure" that their offsprings succeed.

The Judge's "Good Intentions" backfire into the "Sit Down Strike" of the demoralized child.

Parents sometimes say, "It would be nice to let our children take their time, but look at the competition. There isn't time for the luxury of finding oneself. I have to push, or they might not get into a good college. This is going to determine the kid's life."

In *Profound Simplicity,* Will Schutz was faced with something of this dilemma when his son Caleb decided to drop out of high school. To his father's objections, Caleb challenged, "And you said people should follow their own energy. I have no energy for school. I hate to go to school. But I stay up until two in the morning working on this job I have. And I go bowling every night." Schutz realized that for all his intellectual acceptance of the benefits of following one's own energy, on the gut level he had difficulty with his son's decision. "My belief in the principles I championed extended from the top of my head down to about my throat," Schutz admitted.

Later, Schutz brought his readers up to date:

What became of Caleb? He dropped out of school, his business venture failed, and he started hanging out at bowling alleys. As a result, he became a premier bowler. Then he tired of the whole thing. On his own initiative, he began studying for the high school equivalency exam, passed it, and went to junior college a year and a half ahead of his high school class. He paid for part of his education from his winnings in bowling tournaments. He transferred to the University of California, Santa Cruz, graduated with honors, and was admitted to graduate school at UCLA.

Caleb's decision, which most certainly would be considered "wrong" by the Judge of most people, worked out surprisingly well. And what if Caleb had not returned to college? Chances are that he would have been satisfied in his work or bowling venture, so where's the problem? Many young people have no commitment to college at age 18. In fact, many would do much better going at a later date, when they could bring some real life experience and an increased sense of self awareness to bear upon the subject matter pursued.

Making the Commitment

After spending the entire winter going from one cold to another, and having all of my ski holidays disappear into a box of tissues, I made the decision that I did not have to kill myself through overwork. This decision was not made instantly, or easily. Dire self-warnings like, "You'll lose it all if you don't keep going," cropped up frequently. Moreover, my increased free time necessitated a new look at myself. My recognition that my body was telling me something through my constant colds, and that if I didn't listen, I would have to give myself a stronger message, led me to revise my schedule. Being self-employed, I have had the freedom to adjust my activities. The fact that I was working more than any standard job required simply demonstrated the demands of my own Judge.

Even if you are not free to change the actual external time structure of your position, your level of stress can still be drastically reduced. Joyce, for example, told me that she no longer has headaches while working in her office. By turning off her incessant *Be Perfect* Driver, Joyce found that she was much more relaxed. Her first realization that perhaps she didn't have to *Be Perfect* came when she sent a letter to her sister. On the envelope she had crossed out an error instead of rewriting the entire address again. When she cautiously commented on her mistake, her sister candidly admitted that she hadn't even noticed. "That's what convinced me," Joyce stressed, "that my perfection was not only too costly, but also unnecessary."

Only when damaging Imposed Self messages have been diffused can the Intrinsic Self fully emerge. This emergence will occur automatically and naturally when the oppressive weight of the Judge is not constantly bearing down, demanding that we strive for status, money, success, fame or even for love.

Several weeks ago, I moved one of my plants, which had grown to nearly ceiling height, to another less conspicuous area. Although it had not actually been touching the ceiling, it had stopped growing. Within a couple of days, the plant sent out a profusion of new shoots, which were actually twice as large as those that had come before.

Just like my plant, given the additional room necessary to move beyond your oppressive Judgmental Structure, you too will spontaneously generate entirely new aspects of yourself. You will experience an abundance of new energy, new ideas, and new growth.

Within the growth model that you are embracing, you may take drastic steps to change your living situation. You may move to a new place or redecorate your old one. You may find new working hours, a new profession, renegotiate with your partners and friends, or establish new connections. These visible changes will reflect your increased awareness of your inner self-talk. At long last, you will claim and enforce your just title to yourself. In establishing a property right to **you**, you are affirming, "First and foremost, I belong to me!"

Accept yourself as you really are. Reject your obsolete limitations. Realize your authentic self. Live your creativity, energy and aliveness. Change your self-talk. Create your brand new life.

BIBLIOGRAPHY

Apfelbaum, Bernard, Martin Williams, and Susan Greene. *Expanding the Boundaries of Sex Therapy.* Berkeley, CA: Berkeley Sex Therapy Group, 1979.

Bach, George, and Peter Wyden. *The Intimate Enemy.* New York: Morrow, 1969.

Barbach, Lonnie Garfield. *For Yourself: The Fulfillment of Female Sexuality.* New York: Signet, 1976.

Beck, Aaron, John Rush, Brian Shaw, and Gary Emery. *Cognitive Therapy of Depression.* New York: The Guilford Press, 1979.

Bem, Sandra. "Androgyny vs. The Tight Little Lives of Fluffy Women and Chesty Men", *Psychology Today,* September 1975, pp. 58-62.

Berne, Eric. *What Do You Say After You Say Hello?* New York: Grove Press, 1972.

Branden, Nathaniel. *The Disowned Self.* New York: Bantam, 1973.

Bradshaw, John. *Healing the Shame that Binds You.* Deerfield Beach, FL: Health Communications, 1988.

Bukkyo Dendo Kyokai. *The Teaching of Buddha.* Tokyo: Toppan Printing, 1987.

Butler, Pamela E. *Self-Assertion for Women,* Revised ed. San Francisco: HarperCollins, 1992.

Cousins, Norman. *Anatomy of an Illness.* New York: Norton, 1979.

Cummings, Nicholas. "Turning Bread into Stones", *American Psychologist,* December 1979, pp. 1119-29.

Donahue, Phil & Company. *Donahue: My Own Story.* New York: Simon & Schuster, 1979.

Ellis, Albert. *Reason and Emotion in Psychotherapy.* New York: Lyle Stuart, 1976.

Fasteau, M. *The Male Machine.* New York: McGraw-Hill, 1974.

Friedman, Meyer, and Ray Rosenman. *Type A Behavior and Your Heart.* New York: Fawcett Crest, 1974.

Fritz, Sara. "New Breed of Workers", U.S. *News & World Report,* September 3,1979, pp. 35-38.

Gallwey, Timothy. *The Inner Game of Tennis.* New York: Random House, 1974.

Goldberg, Herb. *The Hazards of Being Male.* New York: Signet, 1977.

Gordon, Thomas. *Parent Effectiveness Training.* New York: Peter H. Wyden, Inc., 1970.

Goulding, Mary, and Bob Goulding. *Changing Lives Through Redecision Therapy.* New York: Brunner/Mazel, 1979.

Hawthorne, Nathaniel. "The Birthmark", *Nathaniel Hawthorne's Short Stories.* New York: Knopf, 1946.

Hite, Shere. *The Hite Report.* New York: Dell Publishing Company, 1977.

Hokanson, J., and R. Edelman. "Effects of Three Social Responses on Vascular Processes", *Journal of Personality and Social Psychology,* 3, (1966), 442-47.

Homey, Karen. *Neurosis and Human Growth.* New York: Norton, 1950.

Johnson, Wendell. *People in Quandaries.* New York: Harper & Row, 1946.

Kahler, Taibi. "Drivers: The Key to the Process of Scripts.", *Transactional Analysis Journal* 5, no. 3, (July, 1975), 280-84.

Kamin, Ira. "Dropping the Smile for Awhile", *California Living Magazine, San Francisco Examiner and Chronicle,* January 21, 1979, pp. 6-8.

Karpman, Steven. "Fairy Tale and Script Drama Analysis", *Transactional Analysis Bulletin,* 26, (April 1968), 39-43.

Keller, Suzanne. "The Female Role: Constants and Change", *Women in Therapy,* ed. V. Franks and V. Burtle, pp. 411-34. New York: Brunner/Mazel, 1974.

Kearns, Doris. *Lyndon Johnson and the American Dream.* New York: Harper & Row, 1976.

Korzybski, Alfred. *Science and Sanity,* 2d Ed. Lancaster: Science Press, 1941.

Laxer, Robert M. "Relation of Real Self-Rating to Mood and Blame and their Interaction in Depression", *Journal of Consulting Psychology*, 28, (1964), 38-46.

Lazarus, Richard S. "Positive Denial: The Case for Not Facing Reality", *Psychology Today*, 13, no. 6 (November 1979), 44.

Lear, Martha Weinman. *Heart Sounds*. New York: Simon & Schuster, 1980.

LeShan, Eda. "I'll Never Be Fat Again", *Woman's Day*, July 17, 1979, p. 101.

Luthman, Shirley. *Collection 1979*. San Rafael, CA: Mehetabel & Company, 1980.

Mahoney, M. and C. Thorensen. *Self-Control: Power to the Person*. Monterey, CA: Brooks/Cole, 1974.

Maslach, Christina. "Burned-Out", *Human Behavior* (September 1976), 16-22.

Masters, William, and Virginia Johnson. *Human Sexual Inadequacy*. Boston: Little, Brown, 1970.

McKuen, Rod. "I'm Strong But I Like Roses", *Each of Us Alone*. Burbank, CA: Warner Brothers/Seven Arts Records.

Meichenbaum, Donald. *Cognitive-Behavior Modification*. New York: Plenum Press, 1977.

Melvin, Kenneth B., F. Thomas Cloar, and Lucinda S. Massingill. "Imprinting of Bob White Quail to a Hawk", *Psychological Record*, 17 (1967), 235-38.

Milgram, Stanley. *Obedience to Authority*. New York: Harper & Row, 1975.

Miller, Alice. *For Your Own Good*. New York: Farrar, Straus & Giroux, 1983.

Miller, Alice. *Thou Shalt Not Be Aware*. New York: Farrar, Straus & Giroux, 1984.

O'Neil, Nena, and George O'Neil. *Open Marriage*. New York: Avon, 1972.

Perls, Fritz. *Gestalt Therapy Verbatim*. Lafayette, CA: Real People Press, 1969.

Pirsig, Robert M. *Zen and the Art of Motorcycle Maintenance*. New York: Bantam, 1979.

Powelson, Harvey. Personal communication.

Powys, Llewelyn. "Letter to Warner Taylor" In *The Creative Process*, Brewster Ghiselin. New York: Mentor Books, 1955.

Rossman, Martin. *Healing Yourself.* New York: Pocket Books, 1989.

Rubin, Lillian. *Women of a Certain Age.* New York: Harper & Row, 1979.

Ryan, Cornelius, and Kathryn Morgan Ryan. *A Private Battle.* New York: Fawcett Popular Library, 1979.

Schutz, Will. *Profound Simplicity.* New York: Bantam, 1979.

Selye, Hans. *The Stress of Life.* Revised Edition. New York: McGraw Hill, 1978.

Simonton, O. Carl, Stephanie Mathews-Simonton, and James Creighton. *Getting Well Again.* New York: Bantam, 1980.

Steinem, Gloria. "Erotica and Pornography: A Clear and Present Difference", *Ms. Magazine,* November 1979, p. 53.

Speer, Albert. *Inside the Third Reich.* New York: Avon, 1970.

Teale, Edwin Way. *The Wilderness World of John Muir.* Boston: Houghton Mifflin, 1954.

Tennov, Dorothy. *Super Self: A Woman's Guide to Self-Management.* New York: Jove Publications, 1977.

Weinberg, Harry. *Levels of Knowing and Existence.* New York: Harper & Row, 1976.

Woolf, Virginia. *Professions for Women.* Quoted in Tillie Olsen, *Silences.* New York: Delacorte Press, 1978.

"Your Pursuit of Happiness", *Psychology Today* (August 1976): 31.

Zilbergeld, Bernie. *Male Sexuality.* New York: Bantam, 1978.

ABOUT THE AUTHOR

Dr. Pamela Butler is a clinical psychologist in private practice in Mill Valley, California. She has an active practice, seeing individuals, couples, families, and groups. Using Cognitive Behavioral Therapy principles, Dr. Butler treats problems ranging from depression to phobias to general anxiety and unhappiness. She is trained and highly skilled in the use of EMDR (Eye Movement Desensitization and Reprocessing) to treat clients with Post Traumatic Stress Disorder. During her thirty-five year career, Dr. Butler has conducted numerous workshops and professional training seminars through both her own practice and through association with the University of California Extension. In addition, she has consulted with and provided training to the management and employees of various corporations, including Westinghouse, Levi Strauss, Macy's, Buttes Gas and Oil Company, and Marsh and McClendon.

Dr. Butler is the author of the bestselling book, *Self Assertion for Women*, published by Harper/Collins (1976), which is currently in print and available through Amazon.com. Dr. Butler wrote *Talking to Yourself* in 1981. It was one of the first books published in the new field of Cognitive Behavior Therapy. *Talking to Yourself* was initially published in hardcover by Stein and Day. Harper/Collins created several subsequent paperback editions, including translations into Chinese and French. This new edition reflects substantial updating and editing in order to make it more readable and applicable to the contemporary reader. Dr. Butler may be contacted at (415) 332-3352.